OVERCOME FEAI

CLAIM YOUR COURAGE

KRYSTAL STEWART

TWO PENNY
PUBLISHING

An imprint of Two Penny Publishing
twopennypublishing.com

For information about the author, book events, or interviews, please contact the author representative at:
info@twopennypublishing.com

Printed in the United States of America
FIRST EDITION

Paperback ISBN: 978-1-950995-55-4
Ebook also available!

Dedicated to my mom
Love, your little dreamer

table of contents

introduction

Stupid me!

I knew something wasn't right. I hadn't been to the doctor for an annual checkup for over eight years.

My husband and I were church planters. We believed in our mission and were deeply dedicated to our cause. After our youngest daughter was born, in order to pay the bills at the church we had just started, I became uninsured and stopped going to the doctor. I mean, who needs regular checkups when you're young and healthy?

Stupid me.

Anytime my husband, Ronnie, and I had extra money, we bought things our church needed or hired more staff. To assist the church financially, Ronnie and I both worked side jobs, and at times would even sell one of our vehicles to make ends meet. Owning a home was out of the question.

Our church had a large food pantry we used to feed those in need in our community. But what most people didn't know was that our family often ate out of our church's food pantry as well. Ronnie and I were both hard workers and knew we could take staff positions at other churches to make more money and make ends meet if we ever had to. In fact, there were several times we got offered full-salaried positions at other churches; but it was never about the money. We believed so deeply in our own church plant, we always declined. Our mission was, *"We don't have to do this; we get to do this!"* It was our choice and an honor serving our community.

Our family shopped primarily at second-hand stores or from the clearance rack section. I tried to make shopping at these kinds of stores trendy and cool — thankfully, our kids thought that's what we were actually doing. In reality, that's all we could afford.

I'm not gonna lie;
we really struggled.

After several years of sacrificing to start our new church, it was finally taking off. We renovated and moved our church into an old grocery store, which was a huge leap from our original meeting space in the food court of a mall. I began hosting and leading quarterly ladies' events with hundreds of women regularly attending. I could fill a book just sharing testimonies of the beautiful things that took place at those ladies' events. They were a dream to be a part of; God never ceased to amaze us as He touched women's hearts those nights. We had almost a full staff; and through our weekly outreach ministry, we fed hundreds of people. And finally, yes finally, Ronnie and I were both receiving a weekly paycheck.

All of our sacrifices were starting to pay off, and it felt good to see breakthroughs in the church and in the city we loved so much. And it felt really good not to have Ramen Noodles on the menu so often.

My personal ministry was also taking off. I was speaking at other Christian ministry events and even made my first appearance on a national Christian television show.

The ministry flourished off of miracles, as even someone without faith would have a hard time denying the stories as such. I recall one of my favorites…

In our first year as, what some would call us, a 'baby church,' we were running between 25-50 people and had felt the need to do a Back to School Bash for our community. We were still struggling ourselves but pulled our resources together and handed out flyers for a free back to school outreach. We packed 250 backpacks with school supplies to give away, offered free lunch, and partnered with a few local barbers and hair stylists that were giving free haircuts to the kids to get ready for school.

Just 30 minutes before the event was scheduled to begin, Ronnie nervously said to me, *"Krystal, I really hope people show up today, and we are not left with all these backpacks!"* No more than five minutes later one of our volunteers ran up to us, *"Hey, guys, I think you better come see this!"*

We went to the front door to see what he was looking at; our eyes widened, and we gasped in disbelief, as we stared at 500 people lined up down the street waiting for the event to begin. By the time we started we had over 1,000 people at an event which we planned for 250;

and by some miracle I can only compare to the Bible's fish and loaves story, we had enough hotdogs to feed everyone! The backpacks ran out quickly; however we made an announcement for any kids who missed out to write their names down, and we would that following Sunday give them a backpack full of school supplies. The announcement sounded right at the time, until we got in the car exhausted after the event and picked up the list to see we needed 500 more backpacks. We had no idea how we were going to come up with the funds within 48 hours, but decided we would not allow this to ruin our celebration of the day. We posted the pics and videos of the event online thanking our volunteers who had worked so hard.

Within an hour of posting, a pastor friend of ours texted Ronnie saying, "Hey, Ronnie, I saw your event today. How many more backpacks do you need?"

We were confused by his text because we did not mention the fact we had run out of backpacks and had a list of 500 kids who were planning to show up in 48 hours. How did he know? No one knew! Ronnie decided to answer the question and responded, "I need 500 by Sunday; how did you know?"

He sent back a smiley face emoji and replied, "I had the same thing happen to me many years ago at an event and knew as soon as I saw your pics. I will have a check in my mailbox for you within an hour to cover what you need."

And just like that we had
500 more backpacks...

The dream God placed in our hearts to be a Refuge to our hurting community was happening before our eyes; and the scripture we stood on was from *Psalm 46:1, God is our Refuge and strength, a very present help in times of trouble.*

The first year Ronnie and I could afford health insurance, we bought it. After eight years, I finally found myself sitting in a doctor's office. There I sat telling myself I had nothing to worry about. I was young and healthy, right?

The doctor came in and gave me a physical, including a routine pap smear—no big deal.

Stupid me.

A few days later, Dr. Nwosa's office called and asked me to come back in. So there I sat, once again, waiting. Finally, my doctor came in; and after some small talk, she calmly said, "Krystal, I'm not sure what it fully means, but your pap smear is abnormal." "We need to do a biopsy." What did she just say? Do a biopsy? Really? Are you sure?

Honestly, I was both surprised and not surprised because a few times before going in for my checkup, I heard God's still-small voice nudging me in that direction, "Krystal, go to the doctor." So I wasn't overly surprised they had found something; but although I had faith, I was still shocked and scared.

Dr. Nwosa gave me the option to wait three months and do the pap smear again; but since I had already felt that something wasn't right and had already sensed God's nudging me in this direction, I scheduled my biopsy on the spot.

Two weeks later, I went in for the biopsy. It was a simple procedure, but the impact of what the results would show could be life changing; and I knew it. An entire week of anxiety, wondering, worrying, and a lot of prayer went by before I found myself, once again, waiting in my doctor's office. Dr. Nwosa came in and got right to business. She read me the biopsy report.

I had cervical cancer.

Ok, let's pause right here, friends, because we are just getting to know each other; and I just dropped this *major life bomb* on you. The *C word* right after the amazing backpack story, but that's exactly how I felt. Like a bomb went off in the room, and I didnt even know I was in a war zone! Has that ever happened to you? It was the best of times and the worst of times, all at the same time? That's exactly what was happening to me at this moment, and it took me a few seconds to process what had just happened. Ok, let's continue...

Cue ears ringing…

"Umm... excuse me, Dr. Nwosa, what did you just say?"

Ronnie and I decided the fewer people who knew, the better. We thought our time of struggle was over and saw this as only a small setback — no big deal. We had already fought poverty for the past eight years; and it was finally breaking, so there was no way we were going to have any more setbacks.

Even though my cancer was in its early stages, I still felt embarrassed. Cervical cancer is one of the most preventable cancers for women, with regular pap smears. Why had I waited so long to go to the doctor for a checkup? What was I thinking?

Our state of poverty had angered me, but this diagnosis of cancer angered me even more. I felt violated. Dirty. Shameful. Along with my shame came the voices in my head shouting out at me, telling me just how stupid I was. I blamed my past choices for what was happening to me. Was this all my fault? Did I not have enough faith? Was it that I didn't pray hard enough? Sickness offended me, and I felt HUMILIATED that it had become part of my story. I started questioning every decision that led me to this point. Why in the world had I dropped out of college and gotten married? For goodness sakes, I wasn't going to become a preacher's wife; I was going to become a doctor! I was going to be the next medical wiz kid. If I just followed the path I had planned for myself as a young college student, this wouldn't have happened. I blamed myself. I couldn't see past this singular moment to everything Ronnie and I believed in, everything we worked for. All I saw was the diagnosis, and I hated myself for it.

Instead, there I sat being told by a doctor (mind you, a doctor my own age) that I was a loser. Of course, she didn't use those words, but that's how I felt—one big, stupid loser.

After Ronnie and I prayed and discussed my different options for treating my cancer, I decided to have a complete hysterectomy. Without my doctor having any recent pap smear reports to compare this to, she was reluctant to just cut out the part of my cervix that could be affected, which is a less invasive option for some women in the early cervical cancer stages. I could go that route if I really wanted to, but Dr. Nwosa did not recommend it. She explained I would need to continue with the regular biopsies and multiple cervix surgeries for months until everything was cleared up and that I had a big chance of ending with a complete hysterectomy. I didn't want the agony of my cervix being butchered slowly as if it were in a butcher shop (sorry for the graphic detail); and I definitely didn't have the time to deal with multiple surgeries, so the decision was made—go big or go home! Heck, no big deal. Get this chapter of my life over with and move on. Within a few weeks, I'll be back to living my dream life again.

Stupid me. Wrong again.

I awoke from my surgery in excruciating pain.

My hysterectomy had been what the doctors called an "open procedure." My abdomen incision is similar to a C-section incision. But for some reason, instead of waking up to a cup of ice chips and the pain from the surgery being numbed by the morphine pump I was attached to, I woke up in excruciating pain. The pain pump didn't feel like it was even working.

I remember my nurse kindly reminding me, "Now, honey, whenever you need some relief, just push this little button here; and it will take care of all your pain." But I was out of my mind in such severe pain that all I could say back to her, as I pushed the button as fast as I could, was, "Please help me! Please help!"

The anesthesiologists rushed in to identify the problem. They determined the pain medicine was being administered properly. Still, for some reason, my body wasn't responding the way it should. They watched as I writhed in pain.

Next, my doctors hurried in to try to figure out what was going on. First, they looked confused, then concerned. I became scared when they looked really concerned.

The next thing I knew I was being wheeled down the hall, put back to sleep, and rushed back into surgery. When I awoke, the doctors told me that, because of the immense pain I was in, my vital signs indicated I was about to have a stroke. Even though I had pushed that pain button over one hundred times a minute (the amount of morphine that would normally knock out a grown man), it wasn't giving my small body as much pain relief as even an aspirin would give.

Through some blood tests, my doctors finally discovered I had an abnormal gene that caused my body to metabolize certain medications differently. That's why the morphine didn't work on me and why my pain was so severe and had caused my body to go into shock. I was now saddled with a continuous catheter nerve block which left tubes coming out of my abdomen as a way to numb the pain.

Again I felt violated. Embarrassed. Ashamed. I just wanted something to be easy. At least let the medicine that was supposed to numb my pain...well, at least let that work.

On my second day in the hospital, still attached to the catheter, and thankfully with the pain better managed, I still knew something wasn't right. I wasn't sure what, but I would soon find out.

In order to avoid the trauma my body would experience after a hysterectomy and to lessen the probability of being pushed into menopause at just thirty-three, the surgeons left me with one ovary. (I lost the other one at 13 years old due to a ruptured cyst. Apparently it was my first period gone wrong—welcome to womanhood!) I was thankful for my doctor's preventive efforts, but still I knew something in my body wasn't right. Was it the result of the trauma I had experienced because of the intense pain the day before? Or was it something else?

On the fourth day in the hospital, Dr. Nwosa came into my room. She kindly asked everyone to leave, closed the door, and pulled up a chair next to me. She took my hand, looked me in the eyes and asked, "Krystal, is everything okay?" You would think I would have burst into tears, but I didn't. I felt dead. It was as if all my emotions had packed up and moved out. There was nothing left in me, and I didn't even seem to care.

Dr. Nwosa explained that one of the complications that can occur after a complete hysterectomy is what they describe as your ovaries "going to sleep." She went on to assure me that within a few days the one ovary I had left would "wake right back up;" and after that, I shouldn't have any further problems.

At the moment, I didn't realize the magnitude of the potential complication my doctor was trying to explain to me. Well, I didn't realize the magnitude until two weeks later. I was trying to get ready for the day and just couldn't do it. It was as if my body just stopped. The next thing I knew, I was lying on my bedroom floor in a fetal position, crying hysterically.

I vaguely remember hearing Ronnie on the phone telling the doctor what was happening and pleading with her that I needed help. Thankfully, Dr. Nwosa told Ronnie to bring me right in. Ronnie rushed me back to her office; and after more tests, it was confirmed that the "sleepy ovary" complication I had been warned of was exactly what had happened. My emotions had awakened all at once — and here I was, one big emotional wreck, literally fighting for my life.

I had always been the strong one. I had always been the one in control. I had always been the one giving care to everyone else. But now, not being able to do something about this physical, mental, and emotional state I was in was horrifying.

Something in me had broken, and I couldn't fix it. All I wanted to do was get better. Forget about this horrible season and get my life back. But that wasn't going to happen — at least not anytime soon. I vividly remember the day in my grief I penned these words in my journal...

Nov 3, 2015,
Lost myself inside myself.

During this same season, the support systems in our church started to crumble. Just before my diagnosis and subsequent surgery, our church had experienced our first season of growth. In reality, we were still a "baby church;" and since most of the people were new to our church and weren't that deeply connected to Ronnie and me yet, it really wasn't a real big surprise when people started leaving.

Some of our closest staff members were also leaving. And even though we had known a few weeks before my surgery that God was shifting some of our team to new positions and new places, the timing was still horrible. When Ronnie and I, as the senior pastors, needed to show our strength and be present to help our church during this critical time of transition—right when we were needed most— is when we were both at our weakest.

The reverse was also true. At a time when we needed the strength and support from our church members, for various reasons, they were leaving us. It was the perfect storm.

I'll admit, our church struggling didn't help me in my own struggle. I was enraged that "our enemy" was taking advantage of us during this time of our greatest weakness. I was angry that I couldn't fight for the ministry Ronnie and I had made so many sacrifices for and loved so much. I was angry at Ronnie. He was angry at me. I was blaming him. He was blaming me. The truth was, we were both hurting and had no one else to take it out on, so we were taking it out on one another. Hurt people, hurt people.

I had thought my original plan of having a complete hysterectomy would take care of all the cancer cells and no further treatments would be needed. And even though the surgery had been more difficult than I thought, I was looking forward to recovering from this horrible surgery and getting my life back. If I could just get well, get my strength and sanity back, then Ronnie and I could jump back into ministry and continue on the upward path we had been on.

Stupid me! Wrong again.

I was scheduled for a routine six-week post-op visit — no big deal. Ronnie dropped me off at my appointment, and I headed in to see Dr. Nwosa. She told me she had never seen a morphine pump not work on a patient. She told me how sorry she was for the trauma I had experienced. We said we were both glad it was all over. She also told me how impressed she was that I was turning the corner and getting back into the swing of things with the hormone medication I had started.

I was getting ready to leave when Dr. Nwosa said, "Krystal, I think I already have your surgical report back. Why don't you go ahead and get dressed and then meet me in my office in a few minutes? I'll let you know the results of your report, and that way you won't have to come back next week." I got dressed thinking I'm so glad this horrible season is finally over.

I walked into my doctor's office and sat down across from her at her desk. She was reading through the report when I noticed her eyebrows begin to scrunch. She had a look of confusion which quickly shifted to a look of concern. I heard her sigh as she put the papers down, looked at me, and said, "Krystal, I'm so sorry, but your surgical report indicates you don't have clear margins, which means you're going to need further treatment." Thoughts in my head started screaming. This has to be a mistake. This can't be right. Further treatments? What does that even mean?

My doctor told me I would need to schedule a time to see an oncology specialist; and after they reviewed my report, they would discuss my options for further treatments. Then she said, "To be honest, you'll probably need another surgery, plus chemo and radiation." I felt the room spinning. I wanted to puke. I gathered myself long enough to blurt out, "I already had a complete hysterectomy! What further surgery could they even possibly do to me?"

I'll spare you the horror of the details she described, but let's just say it was highly likely that the next round of treatments would ruin my sex life forever. I immediately had questions swirling in my mind about my marriage and the fact that I was only thirty-three. Only thirty-three years old!

I felt my anger turning to rage.

I walked out of the doctor's office completely horrified. I couldn't stop crying. A flood burst, gushing out like an uncontrollable torrent. In the midst of my runaway emotions, I thought of my husband Ronnie and decided I didn't want him to have to deal with this mess of mine. This was embarrassing! And it was my problem. Not his. I decided it would be best if we just split. This was the last thing my marriage needed as tension had already been at an all-time high. Call it fight or flight hormones, stubbornness, or just plain pride, but I was not going to feel like a victim or a problem my husband had to take care of. Instead, I decided I was going to set him free and give him a way out! You know, reject him before he could reject me? (Don't judge me, it sounded like a great idea at the time.) I stopped crying, put on my stern, serious, face and looked him straight in the eyes and said, "Ronnie, I don't want you to do this with me. And honestly I'd rather do it alone. I think it's best if we just go our separate ways now."

Insert dramatic pause…

Except nothing dramatic happened. It didn't even phase him! He chuckled like I had just told him a joke and said, "That's ridiculous! We're not going down that defeated path. We've already been through too much to give up now. We're going to fight this thing together."

And, fight we did.

PRAYER

As a little girl I always had a very intimate prayer life with God. I would write God letters and secretly blow Him a kiss goodnight! I've never felt rejected or judged by God, only by people. You can talk to God without any fear of being hurt. It's your secret place. It's the one place you can be completely vulnerable.

That's why at the end of each chapter I want to give you the opportunity to pray with me. I want to do this with you believing it will be a beginning for you to open up and share your deepest needs and your dearest dreams with God.

> *HEY GOD, IT'S ME.*
> *Thank you for allowing me to be honest with you about what I'm feeling right now and knowing you are there to listen. I pray you give me the strength and wisdom I need to face everything I am dealing with in this season.*
> *Love, Me.*

chapter one

RAGE CAME FIRST

In the days and weeks following the hysterectomy and ongoing treatments for cancer, rage took over. You've probably heard the expression, "Don't poke the bear" or "She went all momma bear on me." Well, that's what happened with me.

In my past I had never allowed "momma bear" to come out unless I was defending my kids. If someone, or even the devil, was messing with me, I somehow thought that *allowing myself to be angry and fight back would be a sin. As a good Christian woman, shouldn't I just keep my mouth shut and deal with it? Doesn't being a real Christian mean you let yourself be run over again and again and again?* Not sure when that stinking-thinking came into my head, but I now realize just how damaging and destructive that kind of thinking really is.

Stupid me.

After I had cancer, all that changed. I felt anger like I'd never felt before! I was angry at every person who had ever hurt me. I was angry at people who had bullied me. I was angry at people who had held me back. I was angry at Ronnie. And I was angry at myself!

In the past I had used anger to fight for other people: a friend, a family member, a church member, or a fellow colleague. And in my religious box, in my Christian circle, it was okay to feel anger for others. It was socially acceptable. But with a cancer diagnosis, things shifted for me. For the first time in my life, Momma Bear came out; and I was fighting for me. There was only one problem with that; in my religious box, that kind of anger — anger used for your own self — wasn't okay!

Rage Is Tricky

I understand why people don't know what to do with rage when it shows up. I certainly didn't. It's erratic and makes you feel out of control. It can be scary to see from the outside and also a little bit scary to feel on the inside. Little did I know that rage would be a gift to me; a God-given gift.

Let me explain.

I have always believed rage is a sin as Ephesians 4:21 says, *"Get rid of all bitterness, rage and anger."* So you can imagine my horror when it reared its ugly head in my life! Growing up I was taught to repress rage. If you want to be a really good Christian, do everything you can to hide it, mask it with something else. You can be needy and clingy but not express rage. No way! I had been taught that rage was an emotion I shouldn't embrace. It was too wild. It was too risky. But I have realized you can't get rid of something if you don't know where it goes and as strange as it may seem, rage became part of God's plan for me.

The Beginning Of Courage Is Rage

Here's how.

You see, growing up as a pastor's kid and then becoming a pastor's wife, it didn't take me long to realize religion was going to be hard work. Those judging me for not dreaming of becoming a pastor's wife when I grew up can probably trace that back to a few ingrained memories from my childhood. It seemed my mom was always being judged for something. I once remember her working all night cleaning the church and redecorating the lobby as a surprise to the congregation before Sunday's service. She worked so hard and came into church the next day excited to share the surprise, only to hear a group of ladies complaining loudly, "Can you believe it? The pastor's wife hung up pictures of pornography in the church!" Actually the picture they were referencing had angels that were wearing loincloths. You know, a loincloth? The same thing Jesus wears in almost EVERY picture of Him hanging on the cross! It's pretty funny telling the story now, but can you imagine how mortifying that accusation would be? My mom cried, she was so humiliated! And then you have my older sister who got pregnant her first time having sex at the age of sixteen. The church demanded she stand in front of the congregation on a Sunday morning alongside her boyfriend and offer an apology for having sex out of wedlock. My father still apologizes to my sister for that day and wishes he hadn't allowed it to happen. But I saw what happened if you tried too hard or messed up, and I didn't want to make the same mistakes. People didn't want the real you; they wanted the perfect you! Or else they would publicly shame and humiliate you. I learned early on I would need to work hard to just blend in. Keep quiet. Don't make any waves. Be nice. So I did, and I did it well.

I also thought being a good Christian woman meant allowing yourself to be bullied. Just let people pretend to be your friends, greet you at church with a smile, gossip behind your back; and you just smile, wave, and walk away. Doesn't a "good Christian woman" need to be quiet and shy, always say yes, suppress her emotions, keep her opinions to herself? Doesn't a good Christian woman just need to stay in the background, have babies and take care of the kids, and, at all costs, avoid making waves?

That's what I thought, so that's what I did.

But after my diagnosis with cancer and my ongoing battle to physically and mentally survive, I started feeling anger like never before. And it wasn't just anger; it was anger turning into outright rage. (In hindsight it was probably a little PTSD and menopause as well, but nonetheless it was real.)

Rage forced me to start asking myself some really hard, brutal, honest questions. Where did this come from? I knew rage was real; it was valid, but I didn't want it to have a lifetime role and knew I needed to do some digging. I started wrestling with many of my repressive, religious belief systems I had had for a long, long time. Was I really meant to just be meek and mild? Was it true I couldn't have personal boundaries? Was it wrong to pursue my own dreams? Was it true that, if I just believed the right things and behaved the right way, everyone would accept me and be pleased with me?

Stupid me.

Fearing people is a dangerous trap,
but trusting the LORD means safety.
Proverbs 29:25

Pretty Faith

As my anger increased and my rage raged, I begged God to help me have what I now call pretty faith. Pretty faith is what I now see as a kind of religion that is nice and neat. Pleasant and proper. Perfect and flawless. It's the way I viewed religion and living my life of service. Blend in, smile, suppress the emotions that make people uncomfortable; but as they ripped organs out of my body, I couldn't find anything pretty about that. As my mental and emotional health unraveled, I didn't find anything pretty about that. As my marriage became tenuous, I didn't find anything pretty about that. Religion wasn't pretty. Repression wasn't pretty. Pretending wasn't pretty. And the direction my life was going certainly wasn't pretty.

First I wanted to hide behind my religious mask. I mean, it was all I knew and how I've lived up to this point. Conceal my negative emotions with positive emotions rather than admitting when I was hurt or angry and dealing with the problem. My coping mechanism worked for many years, but now it had caught up to me.

Honestly, the last thing I wanted to do was act as if everything was okay. "Hey, let's just keep everything neat and nice. Let's just keep playing church. Why don't we just keep talking about casseroles and bake sales. I certainly wouldn't want any of you to feel uncomfortable with me — the obvious mess sitting right here in front of you. Heaven forbid, we wouldn't want that."

Next I wanted to scream.

I wanted to scream as I watched more and more people conveniently walk out of my life. I wanted to scream as I watched my dreams disappear right in front of me. I wanted to scream as my physical, mental, and emotional health continued to unravel into a heaping, ugly mess.

Then I wanted to defend myself.

I wanted to explain to everyone why I was such a mess, but there was one big problem with that. With the side effects of the hormone medication I was taking for early menopause, and with all the stress from the mental, emotional, and physical battle I was dealing with, severe "brain fog" set in; and I couldn't string two coherent sentences together, much less speak in a sane and logical way to defend myself. It was during this season someone left our church because I ignored him. The story goes, he passed me in the hallway and said "hello;" and I snubbed him and just kept walking by. Now I can promise you I would never purposely ignore someone, especially at church. When I heard that dramatic story I lost it! I was barely able to attend church myself, and the last thing I wanted to do was hear how the pastor's wife wasn't measuring up to people's standards anymore and letting the church down.

And finally I just wanted to say, "To hell with it all!"

I didn't have the emotional restraint to fake it anymore. Nor did I want to! I couldn't pretend anymore. I couldn't perform anymore. I couldn't participate in the pretty faith anymore. I was in a battle for my very life; and as much as I wanted my pretty faith to work, it just wasn't working. The prettier I tried to make life, the uglier things got.

What I didn't understand at the time was God was working in a way that stirred something in me that had been lulled to sleep by religion. When God says He will work all things out for our good, this was that. He used my rage to help me break free from a kind of faith that had been sold to me as pretty faith. That false, pretty faith had to go. It hindered my spiritual growth and clouded the vision of the person who was made in God's image. I needed to find myself through the fog, so I opened myself to rage to find out why it was there. At this point I realized all my efforts of getting rid of it were not working, and my only choice was to allow God to reveal the roots of this rage.

> *Now we see things imperfectly, like puzzling reflections in a mirror, but then we will see everything with perfect clarity. All that I know now is partial and incomplete, but then I will know everything completely, just as God now knows me completely.*
> ***1 Corinthians 13:12***

A Good Look In The Mirror

I wasn't angry only at the religious idea of pretty faith, and how it had been used to suppress me; I was also angry at myself. I had become my greatest enemy. I was the hypocrite. I was the one who had picked up the knife slashing away at my dreams. I was the one who had chosen to listen to the voices telling me to settle down, don't be so ambitious; for heaven's sake, Krystal, dream a little less. I was the one who secretly had the word dreamer tattooed in white ink on my left wrist because I didn't want anyone to know I got a tattoo and judge me. I looked in the mirror, and what did I see? I saw an enemy staring back. I saw myself.

Stupid me.

You may be reading this and find yourself saying, "See the church is exactly what I thought, fake people!" or "And that's why I quit going to church because it's a bunch of hypocrites!" and you would be correct.

Yes, there are fake people.

Yes, there are hypocrites.

Yes, the church is imperfect and you want to know how I know that?

Because I go to church and I have been all of those things at one point or another; but here's the rest of the truth: Jesus loves the church and so do I. Jesus loved the church enough to die for it! He actually loves the church so much that He calls it the "Bride of Christ." The church is a family; and I don't know about yours, but I have not yet met a perfect family. There are differences, unnecessary arguments, and sometimes downright nonsense that happens; but there are also miracles, salvation, revivals, healings and some of the most beautiful people in the world. As with any family, you need to know whom to keep boundaries with and whom you can trust. You see, Jesus loves the church but hates religion; and those are two different discussions.

I hate, I despise your religious festivals;
your assemblies are a stench to me.
Even though you bring me burnt offerings and grain offerings,
I will not accept them.
Though you bring choice fellowship offerings,
I will have no regard for them.
Away with the noise of your songs!
I will not listen to the music of your harps.
But let justice roll on like a river,
righteousness like a never-failing stream!
Amos 5:21-24

Now the above Scriptures may seem confusing because God is not against festivals as He said, "Remember the festivals." God is not against singing as He has said, "Sing to the Lord!" But what He is against is when it becomes more about religion and less about Justice and Righteousness. Rather than embracing frightened teenagers facing an unplanned pregnancy, we shame them. Rather than welcoming the sinner, we judge him. We would rather argue with the pastor or the neighboring church rather than uniting to fight the real enemy deceiving the world. We have brothers and sisters in churches all around the world who are being persecuted for being Christians. And when I say persecuted, I am not talking about having their feelings hurt; I am talking about believers who are laying down their lives for the sake of the Gospel. That is the Church we are called to be. Bold, courageous, fighting for injustice and standing up for what we believe. I don't think carpet color or an angel picture in the church lobby fit in those categories; and I decided instead of wasting my time being distracted by the nonsense, I would instead fight for what was important.

Maybe you are here right now in this same place of your life having the same conversation with the enemy in the mirror. You. It's OK! Don't look away. You can't change something you won't confront. I want to challenge you to be vulnerable. God is not judging you! If you're hurt by the church don't be afraid to say you're hurt. God wants to heal your heart, but first you have to admit where you are. Give yourself permission to be exposed and trust that God will finish the good work He has begun in you as He did in me. As controversial as this musical artist is, he sings a song that has always been a favorite of mine.

"I'm starting with the man in the mirror"
Michael Jackson

You see the message is clear. It's easy to blame others or blame the church for making you act a certain way, or give up certain things in your life; but the truth is you are the one who ultimately makes your decisions. Lying to yourself about your feelings will not make them go away (believe me, I tried that). It will just waste your time living a fake life, and is that what you really want at the end of your life? Is that the legacy you want to leave for your children? I didn't. I knew some things needed to change. I had to face the truth about how I felt and give myself permission to address what was and what wasn't working.

Eve, when Satan caused her to doubt herself, also started doubting the character of God, doubting the Word of God, doubting the goodness of God. And now here Satan was all these years later, playing the oldest trick in the book on me.

My self-doubt was leading me to doubt the very character of God, and that doubt was leading me to doubt my very own sense of value and worth. I was wrongly assuming God had made me this way—stupid, insecure, and never good enough—and as a result, I began seeing myself in this wrong way. I was a perfectionist and always felt I was letting Him down. That's not who God is nor how He sees us. We are made in His image, and therefore we have value and worth. Not because of who we are, but because of who He is.

When we give into self-doubt and start living out of low self-worth, we start seeing ourselves as doubters rather than believers, losers rather than winners, followers rather than leaders, slaves rather than sons or daughters. Instead of taking our seat at the "family table," we're content eating in the servant's quarters, because we think that's all we are entitled to.

I needed a new mindset. I needed to see God differently and in turn see myself differently. I needed to remind myself that I did have worth, I did have a future, I did have a purpose. I was a child of God with a good Father. I was a daughter of the King … and I was so much more.

Rage helped me realize I wasn't going to win this battle with a false, pretty kind of faith. I wasn't going to win this battle with a mindset of self-doubt and low self-worth. I needed to embrace my rage, let rage lead me to courage, and let courage help me overcome, not only my battle with cancer, but also to help me break free from all the expectations that had been placed on me and from all the religious boxes I had put over me.

Rage became a gift. It saved my life. It helped me find out who I really was, and not in some selfish, secular, just-gotta-be-me kind of way—but who I was in Christ. Rage also helped me discover what God had called me to do. Not what others thought I should be or what others wanted me to do, but who God had made me to be, and what God had created me to do.

> *I praise you because I am fearfully*
> *and wonderfully made.*
> ***Psalms 139:14***

I began to realize that pretty faith wasn't going to win this battle. I had to let God use rage to rid me of religion, rid me of fear, rid me of faking it, rid me of self-doubt, rid me of passivity, rid me of unbelief. I had to let God use rage to lead me into this new healing, freeing, exciting, adventure He was taking me on. That's the only way it was going to happen.

I knew I wanted to embrace this new life, but first I had to die.

PRAYER

Heavenly Father,

Thank you for reminding me I was created to live a life, not full of fear, but full of freedom. But to do so, God, I need your help. Help me let go of some of the people who have walked out of my life, but not out of my heart. Set me free from my need for approval and acceptance from other people. Instead, let me hold YOU even tighter on this adventurous journey You've created for me. Ignite my dreams again. Remind me that I can do ALL things through You, and Your strength.

Today, I take off all the limits that I've allowed people to place on me. Instead, I'm leaping fearlessly into my destiny. No matter how large the waves may be, give me your courage to walk on top of my circumstances. I'm no longer holding back. I'm moving forward fearlessly into your arms.

Love,

Your fearless child

Quotes to Remember:

> You can't get rid of something if you don't know where it goes.

> The beginning of courage is rage.

> Fearing people is a dangerous trap,
> but trusting the LORD means safety.
> *Proverbs 29:25*

chapter two

THE DAY I BEGAN DYING

My hysterectomy was scheduled for a Tuesday; and the one thing I couldn't get out of my mind the night before my surgery was the morning of my thirty-third birthday, eleven months earlier. I remember waking up that birthday morning and running downstairs to have some study time with God before the rest of the house woke up. I had been researching *amazing things that had happened to people at the age of thirty-three,* and one of the things I had discovered was that Jesus was only thirty-three when he died. I didn't think this was a coincidence, so I decided my prayer for the coming year would be *"He must increase, but I must decrease" (John 3:30) KJV.* I repented and asked God to remove any selfish ambitions from my life. More of Him and less of me!

Now here I was eleven months later preparing for surgery — a full hysterectomy; and as I lay in bed that evening I was utterly confused. *"Um… God, did you take my prayer this last year literally? I mean surely you didn't think I really wanted to die!"* Here I was, eleven months after I dedicated that prayer to the year, and I'm getting ready to undergo major surgery. Was this how God was going to bring me home? Was this *really* my time? I wasn't ready to die.

I didn't know then what I know now, but I was already dying! Not a physical death, but still a real death. I was about to die to the person I had unknowingly become and die to the kind of life I had grown uncomfortably comfortable with.

> *For whoever wants to save their life will lose it, but whoever loses their life for me will find it.*
> ***Matthew 16:25 NIV***

The day I turned 33 — and the very same day I had decided my prayer for the next year would be "*he must increase and I must decrease*" — my parents surprised me with a skydiving experience. I guess you should watch what you pray for!

I had always wanted to know the thrill of jumping out of an airplane, but I had never had the opportunity, nor really ever had the courage to do so. It was on my 'bucket list;' sure, someday I'll do it. Well, thanks to my parents, my 33rd birthday was that day.

I always talked a big game. "Sure, I'd *love* to jump out of a plane. That wouldn't scare me one bit!" I guess my parents were calling my bluff. What I really wanted to tell them was, "I'm scared, really scared. My heart's in my stomach. I don't think I can go through with this." Yet something deep down was beckoning me. My fear wanted to get out, and I wanted to get free. If I backed down now I would be choosing the safe life, burying the adventurer I deeply longed for — possibly abandoning her forever.

For God hath not given us the spirit of fear;
but of power, and of love and of a sound mind.
2 Timothy 1:7 KJV

Since it was my first time skydiving, I was scheduled for a tandem jump. I would be strapped to an instructor who had jumped hundreds of times. After hearing him describe his upcoming jump with me as "just another day in the park," I mustered up enough courage to sign the liability contract, and suited up. I somehow talked my dad into skydiving as well, which is still one of my greatest accomplishments. (Thanks, Dad, you're the best!)

We were now flying 13,500 feet above the ground, where just moments before my feet had been firmly and safely planted. Over the hum of the engine I heard my instructor say, "Krystal, we're up! Take your seatbelt off, come on over here by the door, and let's get ready to jump."

Fear was strapped in the seat next to me.

Would I jump or would I let fear hold me back?

My instructor made it clear he was not allowed to push me if I chickened out (I asked), and the final decision had to be mine.

As my instructor waited at the door, I made my decision. I unbuckled my seatbelt and made my way to the open door. He looked at me and shouted 3, 2, 1; and I jumped. As I took that leap from the aircraft, I let go of fear, grabbed hold of courage, waved goodbye to *pretty faith,* and sailed off into the new adventure God had planned for me.

Would I be the risk taker or the picture taker? What would my story be?

It's clear to me now that my skydiving experience was the beginning of the end for my long-standing friendship with fear. My old way of life — dominated by fear, a false image and my pretty faith — was dying; and my new life, my real life, was just beginning.

Choosing courage that day was monumental for not only me, but everyone around me. Little did I know just how monumental that seemingly simple task would be. Little did I know the incredible amounts of courage I would need in the days and years ahead. This was just the beginning.

Many of you readers have stories of pain and tragedy that mine don't even compare to, and I want you to know I am so glad you are reading this book. Let me just put this disclaimer out there and say I am not comparing *any* of my pain with yours nor my process with your own. My story is not your story; but my prayer is, by sharing how I found the courage to face cancer, religion, my marriage problems, an unplanned adoption (yes, adoption...we will get there and it is an AMAZING story but still took A LOT of courage), and the courage to face the grief from my mom's unexpected death (worst chapter, just giving you a heads up) that something will resonate with you and bring your heart encouragement, or at least entertainment. I know life can have some really horrible seasons, and even right now the world is hurting on so many levels. But I am believing God will use my story for His Glory and something will speak to you in your current season.

Even if it's as simple as my saying,

I Jumped. Peter Jumped. So Can You!

I faced my fear by jumping out of an airplane. Peter faced his by jumping out of a boat.

Here's how the Bible describes the scene.

The disciples had just witnessed Jesus feeding a crowd of five-thousand and now they found themselves smack-dab in the middle of a storm. The Bible says, "He (Jesus) could see that the disciples were straining to row, because the wind was against them" (Mark 6:48 NIV). Sounds like a pretty fierce storm.

It also sounds a lot like life.

One minute we're sailing along minding our own business, eating the leftovers from the miracles we just witnessed, when… BAM … we suddenly find ourselves face to face with a violent storm. Whether it's a diagnosis of a severe illness, the report of a friend's death, or a situation threatening to destroy a family member — like the disciples — we're struggling at the oars just trying to stay alive.

But the story doesn't end there.

While the disciples are fighting for their lives, they see in the distance a man walking on the water. Really? A man walking on the water? Under normal circumstances the disciples could have rationalized away the fact that they were *seeing* a man walking on the water. Isn't that just a hallucination? Has fear — caused by the fierce storm I'm in — made me delusional? Have I dreamed something up in my head in hopes he'll come and save me?

But that's not what the disciples did.

Due to the do-or-die circumstance they were in, they cast their pride aside. Who cares if they look like they're insane. They call out anyway. "Hey over here! We're desperate. We need your help!"

Just because you're struggling doesn't mean you're failing.

Jesus approaches the boat.

But notice: Jesus didn't calm the storm or leap into the boat and comfort them or save them. Instead, He offered the disciples an opportunity to embrace a miracle. Did they want to take a risk and see what might happen? Or did they want to do nothing, stay in the boat, play it safe, and take their chances?

In the midst of our storm, Jesus offers us the same option.

Out of the twelve, only one, Peter, takes up the offer. Only one was willing to let go of fear and grab hold of courage. Peter grabbed hold of courage and asked Jesus the impossible, "If it is You, bid me to come out on the water." Jesus responds, "Come." (Matt 14:28) KJV

In the midst of the storm, eleven of them froze. They chose to stay in a boat that was sinking. They chose to remain in a situation that could quickly, and quite literally, become their tomb. Think about it: they were willing to die rather than take the risk. Many times this same challenge is true for us.

During our most difficult seasons we're given a choice. We can choose the seemingly safer, more popular route. We can allow our doubt, fear, and unbelief to paralyze us. We can stay in the boat and do nothing. Or we can be the one, sometimes the only one, to take hold of courage and choose the adventurous route, the freeing route, the route God has planned for us.

Jesus offers you his extended hand. Will you reach out to him so that you can live, or will you stay in the boat?

What will you choose?

You live only once; be fearless.

Reach For His Extended Hand

Let me encourage you. Choose courage. Take the risk. Grab hold of Jesus' outreached hand. Decide today that you will *no longer be controlled by fear*. Don't let what people think of you or the power certain people have had over you, hold you back any longer. You only have one life to live, so don't waste another second living in fear. Don't let religion hold you down. Don't let *pretty faith* hold you back. Don't let self-doubt hold you down. Take the seat belt off and head toward the door. Let go of fear. Grab hold of courage, jump...and sail off into the new adventure God has waiting for you.

If this world-wide pandemic has taught us anything it's this: Fear is real and so is courage. Persistent fear negatively affects individuals' decision-making abilities and causes anxiety, depression, and poor physical health. Here we are being afraid of Covid-19 not realizing the fear itself is lowering our immune system and making us more susceptible to sickness. Now I am not saying that Covid-19 is not real; I have unfortunately had many people that I love be affected by it. My father spent time in the hospital with this horrible virus, and I have friends who have lost loved ones; and *it has been devastating.* But I am saying you cannot stop living in the wake of this danger. If you keep waiting for the fear to leave for you to step into your dreams, you are going to run out of time. It's time to divorce fear and end the toxic relationship!

Now LEAP, dear one;
you were created to fly!

PRAYER

Dear Heavenly Father,

Please give me the courage today to take the step of faith I have been afraid to take. I know you created me for a purpose, and I don't want that purpose to be unfulfilled due to fear in my life. Today I choose to end my relationship with fear and step out in faith regardless of how large the waves may seem. I trust your voice and I'm ready to take the first step toward those dreams you have placed in my heart. Ready or not, here I come!

Love,

Your Courageous Child

Quotes to Remember:

You live only once; be fearless.

Just because you're struggling
doesn't mean you're failing.

Will you be the risk taker or the
picture taker?

For God hath not given us the spirit of
fear; but of power, and of love
and of a sound mind.
2 Timothy 1:7 KJV

chapter three

I still find it humorous that "Barbie Girl" was what I became known as. Blonde. Cute. Petite. Proper. I hated that pretty and perfect perception placed on me. After I had cancer, I hated my "Barbie Girl" image even more.

First of all, that's not who I was. Ever.

My sister played with Barbies, not me. You would find me in the basement with boxing gloves sparring with my brother, or covered in grease in the garage working under a car with my father. While most little girls were dreaming of being a princess, I was dreaming of being a firefighter, or a policeman, or like my older brother, dreaming of joining the AirForce.

I also hated the Barbie Girl label because it was often used against me. People projected this image on me as a way to bully me; as a way to push me into what they expected of me. They also used it as a way to disqualify me. Surely, as a woman, I shouldn't stand in front of men and preach and teach God's word. Surely women shouldn't do that.

Just be pretty. Be proper. Look nice. Just represent us well by being our pastor's perfect "trophy wife."

Eventually I grew tired of pushing the image away, and I gave in. I played the Barbie Girl part, which made me hate the fake image even more! Over time, my identity and security became wrapped up in this perfect pretty-girl image. Admittedly, my long blonde hair, attention to fashion, and inordinate love for shoes only reinforced this Barbie doll image. But, you know, what polished and promoted this image even more was the fact that I constantly presented my marriage, my family, and my ministry as pretty and perfect. You know like everyone does on social media? The filters, perfect family pictures, perfect children; and we all know about the social media highlight-reel effect, Right? People actually feel depressed after spending a great deal of time on Facebook or Instagram because they feel bad when comparing themselves to others. This may lead us to think their lives are better than they actually are and conversely, make us feel worse about our own lives. But guess what, social media is not real life. No one has a perfect life or a perfect family no matter what they portray.

Once again, I was my own enemy.

Not only did I play this Barbie doll show and intentionally portray it to others, I was also teaching it to other women. Most of my sermons were about "pretty faith." Seldom did I speak about our brokenness or our pain or our scars. Seldom did I speak about the mess and ugliness of life.

It was good for me to be afflicted so that
I might learn your decrees.
Psalm 119:71 NIV

During my battle with cancer, all of this changed.

I began to see my Barbie doll image for what it was; fake and fragile. It wasn't really me, but a false-self of me I had created. An image I had painted, picked up and put on that didn't reflect who I really was. God, in His goodness, began breaking me down so He could build me back up. Through the gift of rage, I broke out of my Barbie doll image and finally figured out who I really was.

Why Even Fight?

I'm constantly amazed by the simple life lessons I've learned from observing my children. My newest epiphany on discovering who I really was came while I was parenting my son, Dallas. When Dallas was three, his favorite word was "Why?" It didn't matter what the statement was, I still got the same response…

Dallas it's time to go to bed, *Why?*
Dallas come and get in your car seat, *Why?*
Dallas it's time to put your shoes on, *Why?*

Sometimes I'd answer, "It's time for bed because the sun has gone to sleep and our bodies are tired." Or, "You need to get in your car seat because 'Mr. policeman' wants you to be safe." Or "You need to put your shoes on so we can go to the store and get some ice cream." Of course, sometimes I would pull out the old parent's trump card and in exasperation say, "Because I said so!"

What I finally realized is that Dallas wasn't trying to be difficult just to be difficult. Instead, his little three-year-old brain was simply trying to figure out the answer to *why we do what we do.*

> Define your why, and it will empower you to fight and fulfill your dreams.

Similar to Dallas at the time, very few people know WHY they do what they do. Every person on the planet knows WHAT they do. This is my job. These are the functions I fulfill. These are the products I sell. These are the services I provide.

We also know HOW we do what we do. I make six sales calls a day. I enter data on the computer for my company. I train people on how to do sales. These are all examples of how I do what I do. But many of us don't know WHY we do what we do.

During my battle with cancer, while facing multiple setbacks, I realized I had to figure out my WHY. I knew if I was going to let rage break me out of my Barbie doll house, I would have to dig deep and find out who I truly was and what God really wanted me to do. I needed to find my true me. I needed to know my WHY.

Life was too painful to just keep going through the motions. If I was going to continue to fight, if I was going to continue to live, I had to find my WHY. Why had God put me on the planet? What was my reason for existing? Who did God want me to further become, and what did God want me to further accomplish?

Dreams: God Are You Sure?

I remember the first time I knew God was "speaking to me" regarding *His* dreams for my life. I wish I could tell you I was "over the moon ecstatic" about these awesome dreams; but to be honest, I wasn't. God's idea of me being a writer and speaker, who was married to a pastor, well…none of these would have been my first choice. Honestly, I'm not sure they were even on my list at all. (Remember the angels in loincloths?)

As a young girl I was a competitive figure skater and dreamed of one day traveling and performing with Disney On Ice. Another dream I had was to become a doctor. This wasn't only a dream for me; I actually started making plans to become a doctor by gaining experience early on. While still in high school, I received my degree as a medical assistant and began working in the hospital for Dr. Simmons and Dr. Simmons-Watson, a surgeon and anesthesiologist who were siblings.

Evidently, God had a different dream for me.

The verse below describes it perfectly, as I felt completely unqualified for the dreams God was showing me, since they were also completely out of my comfort zone.

But God chose what is foolish in the world to shame the wise;
God chose what is weak in the world to shame the strong;
1 Corinthians 1:27 ESV

I had zero degrees in creative writing. Zero! I had never even taken an extra course on the topic. English was my worst subject in school. I can't believe I'm telling you this, but my first unedited manuscript I sent in for feedback came back saying *"This reads like it was written by a sixth grader."* Awesome! Just the confidence booster I needed. By the way, I'm sorry for not warning you of that review before you bought the book; now you're stuck with me. And on top of all that, I have the worst handwriting possible. My handwriting works better for being a doctor, than being a writer, that's for sure. Unfortunately, I grew up in a day when teenagers didn't have cell phones. I know, can you believe it? Living without a cell phone? We didn't get to text or email each other, but instead passed notes at school. Oh, the anxiety I still feel when I have flashbacks of needing to respond to a handwritten note! Funny thing is I still hate my handwriting and make Ronnie fill out birthday or wedding cards from our family.

I was "book smart" and loved school. I had what it took to become a doctor. But to become a writer and speaker, now that was a different story. And to become a pastor's wife, "No, thanks!"

Your dream will never go unopposed.

A Speaker

I'll never forget my first official speaking engagement.

As I stepped off the plane en route to the venue where I would be speaking, I was nervous, but confident. I just knew after these ladies heard my message on faith, their lives would be changed forever. Little did I know it was my life that would be forever changed.

I was wearing a brand-new dress and the best-looking stilettos you've ever seen. My hair was curled, and my makeup was perfect; and I had a fresh French manicure. (For a mom with three small children, getting a manicure neeeeever happened.) It was raining outside, but I was determined the weather wasn't going to rain on my parade. I had already picked up the rental car and gazed into the rear view mirror as I pulled into the church parking lot. Under my breath I mumbled, "Lord, help me." I grabbed my Bible and black binder with my sermon notes, threw my shoulders back and, like Wonder Woman entering a fight scene, I walked through the doors of the church.

Praise and worship was almost over. The final song was playing and then I was up! The anticipation was bubbling up in me so much that if I wasn't careful, when I started to speak, my voice would be wavering from sheer excitement. I hung my head down to squeeze in one more "Lord help me," and then it happened. I overheard a woman behind me, with the loudest whisper you've ever heard, say, "Who is our special speaker today?" (Now, don't even try to judge me for eavesdropping, because I know the ears on every single one of you super-elite Christians' heads would have perked up just like mine did!)

I waited for the other person to respond with something like, "Oh, we're so blessed to have Krystal Stewart from Florida with us today! I hear she's awesome!" The only way I can fully describe what happened next was a huge reality check. The next thing I heard brought Wonder Woman crashing down to earth. The other woman responded with, "It's the girl with those fancy shoes…"

"What? Did I hear that right? Those shoes! What's wrong with my shoes? These shoes are amazing! Incredible! Outstanding!" Okay. You have to understand that I'm a little bit of a shoe nut. To put it mildly, I LOVE SHOES.

I took a deep breath. Then the conversation got even better — or you could say, even worse. I shut my eyes and tried to prepare for my introduction, and then I heard one of the ladies respond back to the other, "Geez, is she the cheapest speaker we could get or what?"

OUCH! That hurt. A lot.

Now, I'm not going to lie and say the thought didn't cross my mind to become the first 6-inch-stiletto-heel-wearing marathon runner ever because, believe me, that thought did cross my mind. I didn't care that it was raining outside. I didn't care that my makeup was perfect and my hair flawless. If I'd had more time to ponder the idea of sprinting out of there, I would have been gone. I lifted my head, opened my eyes, and just as I did, I heard my name, "And now please welcome to the stage Krystal Stewart."

My mind was racing. My heart was pounding. I was trying to push the conversation I had just overheard into the back of my mind. I was saying to myself, "You. Can. Do. This. Come on, Krystal, you got this!"

I wish I could tell you as I spoke about Faith — and how no one is ever too old or too young for miracles to happen in their lives — that all the women were blown away by my message. I wish I could tell you that, as I spoke, the two ladies who had said those unkind words about me — and my shoes — got up, ran to the altar and repented.

That would be a great story.

But that's not what happened.

What really happened was the crowd of women didn't even give me a chance. From the moment I took the microphone and started declaring God's promises, I looked into bored, sleepy, apathetic eyes shouting back at me, "You're wasting our time, Shoe Girl." But that didn't deter me.

The more they cleaned out their purses, the harder I preached! I tried to provoke them by saying, "I'm going to have such CRAZY FAITH that although I live a thousand miles away, you're going to see reported in the news one day the amazing things God has done through me!" I went even further, "You can ASK and RECEIVE as well! ASK God to use you however he wants!" I knew what I was preaching sounded dramatic, but I had to say it. I just knew my powerful message on faith was going to open their eyes to the BIG life God had in store for them.

As the worship music softly played behind me, I began the altar call. This will do it. This is when I'll reach them. "If you want God to use you to do something miraculous in your life, and you want to have a FAITH that will rock this world, I want to pray for you.

Anyone out there willing to stand with me and say you are willing to do WHATEVER God asks of you, regardless of how crazy it sounds? Stand up and come on up to the altar!"

Cue: Crickets.

"Anyone?"

Not a single person so much as even flinched. In complete disbelief I closed in prayer, raised my hands and said, "God you can use me for whatever you want! I'm yours! I pray for FAITH to arise in this place." I closed my binder and prepared to dismiss. Then I saw a slight flicker of movement. I thought it might be the two ladies I had overheard earlier, already heading toward the door.

Instead, I saw a lady from the back row getting out of her seat, tears streaming down her face, coming to the front. I knelt down with this brave woman, and she said to me, "I've been to different churches here and there in town, but I've never truly believed; and I've never ever heard a message like what you just preached tonight. Will you pray with me?"

As thankful as I was that this lady had responded, and as honored as I was to pray the sinner's prayer with her, I still couldn't wait to get out of there as fast as I could. My flight was departing soon, so I had a somewhat valid reason to not hang around long. Just the thought of getting out of there and getting on the plane to head home made it a bit easier to keep my fake smile on and give a few faint hugs on my way out.

What a humiliating, dreadful ordeal!

I made it to the airport and headed into the bathroom to call Ronnie; and that's when, like a geyser, it all came gushing out.

Ronnie answered the phone, "Hey, Babe, how'd it go?"

My wall came tumbling down, and I burst into tears. Between sobs, I blubbered, "It was awful. They hated me, I mean really hated me." Ronnie said, "Oh, it couldn't have been that bad." I blurted back, "Yes! It was! I'm never, ever going to speak at another event, ever again. Never!" It was then I heard through the loud speaker my flight was boarding and told Ronnie, "I gotta go; I'll see you soon." I hung up the phone, blew my nose, and quickly took a glance in the mirror to clean up the leftover mascara that had run down my face.

Buckled snugly in my seat on the plane and heading home, I felt completely discouraged. The voice of defeat was lodged deep in my head and drilling down deeper every minute. Thank God, at least I wasn't crying anymore. I couldn't. I was numb. Confused. Frustrated. Angry. In silence I prayed, "God, why did you send me there just to make me look stupid in front of all those ladies? You're the one who gave me this dream to become a speaker. I didn't even want it! Why did you do this to me?"

I waited for His response … silence.

Joseph in a Pit

Joseph has always been my favorite character in the Bible (except of course, Jesus!). Joseph had the perfect life going for him. Well, it was perfect until God gave Joseph a dream.

Genesis chapter 37 tells us about Joseph's dream. It reads:

"One night Joseph had a dream, and when he told his brothers about it, they hated him more than ever. 'Listen to this dream,' he said. 'We were out in the field, tying up bundles of grain. Suddenly my bundle stood up, and your bundles all gathered around and bowed low before mine!' His brothers responded, 'So you think you will be our king, do you? Do you actually think you will reign over us?' And they hated him all the more because of his dreams and the way he talked about them.
"Soon Joseph had another dream, and again he told his brothers about it. 'Listen, I have had another dream,' he said. 'The sun, moon, and eleven stars bowed low before me!' This time he told the dream to his father as well as to his brothers, but his father scolded him. 'What kind of dream is that?' he asked. 'Will your mother and I and your brothers actually come and bow to the ground before you?' But while his brothers were jealous of Joseph, his father wondered what the dreams meant."
Genesis 37:5-11 NLT

Our enemy doesn't want us to move into the dreams God has for us. When we start living out these dreams that God has given us, that's when it seems the enemy resists us the most. I know, for me, when I'm in a season of living with less passion and less purpose, that's when it seems I experience fewer attacks from the enemy. But every time I start to move further into my dreams, that's when I experience the most attacks from the enemy. I know his goal is to stop us; or if he can't do that, he at least wants to do everything he can to slow us down.

One of the ways he does this is by distracting us. He's the great illusionist. He'll keep us distracted on social media all day or get us spending all our time binging series on Netflix. It's when we start believing in ourselves and start taking steps toward our future, that we see obstacles rise up around us. That's just the way our enemy works!

> *For I know the plans I have for you," declares the Lord,*
> *"plans to prosper you and not to harm you,*
> *plans to give you hope and a future."*
> ***Jeremiah 29:11 NIV***

A Writer

Once God began to reveal His dreams for me to become not only a speaker, but also a writer, out of sheer obedience, I launched my first blog. Now, I'll be the first to admit, it wasn't pretty. I've always hated writing — even as a child — and it was evident! It's rather embarrassing to re-read some of my earliest blogs. Honestly, they weren't that good.

But something unexpected happened.

With so many incredible bloggers out there, I was quite surprised when people started following my blog. Somehow my vulnerability attracted fellow dreamers. While I had my online tribe encouraging to me, I also had my critics. And, sadly, any criticism I received only magnified my insecurities. And yet I continued to write.

I was at a ladies conference called *It's Time to Dream Again* where I first shared my vision of writing a book. The conference was with a group of ladies from our church, so most of them were following my blog and could clearly see that writing wasn't my greatest gift. At the time, the dream of writing a book didn't seem very promising; but I stepped out in faith and told them my dream anyway.

I should have known better. Like Joseph, you have to be careful whom you tell your dreams to.

Watch To Whom You Tell Your Dreams

Joseph had to fight for his dreams, and so will you. His story continues in Genesis 37:

> *"When Joseph's brothers saw him coming, they recognized him in the distance. As he approached, they made plans to kill him. "Here comes the dreamer!" they said. "Come on, let's kill him and throw him into one of these cisterns.*

We can tell our father, 'A wild animal has eaten him.' Then we'll see what becomes of his dreams!"
Genesis 37:18-20 NLT

The enemy sent pain to BREAK you, but instead let it MAKE you.

One of the things I find interesting in the story about Joseph is that Joseph's jealous brothers threw him into an *empty* well. A well isn't dug so that it can be empty. It's meant to be full; full of life-giving water.

Here's why this point is interesting to me.

Could it be that Joseph's brothers were drawn to this *empty* well because it was symbolic of their own lives? Could it be that they weren't living their own dreams? Could it be that their jealousy of Joseph was easy to come rushing in because their own lives were hollow? Their own lives were empty wells? Instead of being filled with words of life to encourage, they were full of jealousy.

Admittedly, we don't know everything about the lives of Joseph's brothers, but we do know about God's character; and we know God didn't create anything without a purpose. I'm confident God had given all of Joseph's brothers dreams for their own lives, yet is it possible that somewhere along the way they stopped fighting for their dreams and instead started making it their mission to fight against the dreams of others?

Until the time came to fulfill his dreams,
the LORD tested Joseph's character.
Psalm 105:19 NLT

Being thrown into an empty well wasn't the only attack Joseph suffered on his journey toward his dream. He also had to deal with being falsely accused and wrongly thrown into prison. He had to rise above accusations, jealousy, and even hate. Joseph had to forgive people many times so he wouldn't become bitter, allowing him to move on and into his dreams. Stop and consider how powerful that choice was. How can you apply that same thinking into your own life? What small act of forgiveness would put you on the path to fulfilling God's plans for your life?

There's a lesson here for all of us.

If you're going to follow the dreams God has put in your heart, you're going to face resistance. People are going to misunderstand you. They're going to be jealous of you. People are going to fight you, but you have to forgive. If you don't, like Joseph's brothers, you'll become your own empty well.

Although we know these attacks against Joseph were ultimately from the enemy, we need to remind ourselves that **God never allows any of our pain to be wasted.** If we'll work with God, as God works with us, He will use our pain for our own good. God used every wrong that was done to Joseph to build his character, to mature him into the man Joseph would need to become. God worked these things into Joseph's life so he would be able to contain, and retain, the place his dreams would later take him. And God will do the same with us.

> *Consider it pure joy, my brothers and sisters, whenever you face trials of many kinds. The testing of your faith produces perseverance. Let perseverance finish its work so that you may be mature and complete, not lacking anything.*
> ***James 1:2 NIV***

This is why I believe Joseph could say, "Bless you, prison!" Because it was in prison where the dreamer inside of Joseph came alive. It was in prison where Joseph's greatest pain pushed him into his greatest destiny. It was in the prison where Joseph found his purpose. It was in prison where Joseph discovered his *Why*.

Like it or not, that seems to be the way God works. He first works in us and then through us. He worked that way in Joseph's life. He worked that way in my life; and, it's my guess, He's at work in that way in your life. God uses our pain to shape us into who He wants us to become and then moves us toward the destiny He has planned for us.

Let me be clear here.

God is not *causing* you pain, but He is *allowing* it in order to refine you and to prepare you for what He has next for you. God knows you can handle it, because it's His strength that's in you. But you also need to know that YOU can handle it. Stand on your platform of pain and let it become your stepping stool. Allow your heart to rage, but make sure it leads you to courage. Don't allow your wounds to turn you into a person you are not. Let it uncover your *Why.* Don't let your anger or rage take you away from your destiny; instead, let it move you into your destiny.

So, to all my fellow dreamers, if you're in a place where you're struggling right now, keep fighting! Where you are is not where you're going to be. Don't get angry at the people around you; get mad at the Dream Thief. He's the one who's trying to rip your dream out of your hands. Let your pain be your weapon and then stand up and use it against him. Let your pain be the fuel you need to keep moving forward!

Pain was the breath that gave life to my dreams.

It's been over ten years, actually closer to 15 years, since I shared at the *It's Time to Dream Again* conference my dream of writing a book. So much has happened since then, and I gave it up many times. I honestly went from loving the dream to hating it as I felt it would never come to pass. Now looking back I can see it was never about me; it was always about God getting the glory for my story. The dream was always ready, but the dreamer still needed more work. Like the saying goes, *No pain, No gain.* So the next time you're experiencing a painful season, be encouraged. Your gain is coming! You're being set up for a miracle. God is working in you during this season. I know, I know. Easier said than done, right? But by His strength, you can do it.

PRAYER

Dream Giver,
I know you have created me for a purpose, and I am asking you to reveal your greater plans for me. Wake me up from just existing and help me become aware of the calling you have for me. Remove the distractions from my life so I can accomplish all you have destined for me! I surrender all the pain I have endured in this lifetime, understanding you can create something beautiful out of my brokenness. Teach me how to love others more deeply and to be present in every moment you have graced me with. I am ready to be your light in this dark world and to SHINE!
Love,
Your Dreamer

Quotes To Remember:

Define your WHY, and it will empower you to fight and fulfill your dreams.

Your dream will never go unopposed.

The enemy sent you pain to break you, but instead let it make you.

God never allows any of our pain to be wasted.

Your pain is your weapon.

Discovering your WHY will give you the courage to overcome any challenge opposing your dream.

Until the time comes to fulfill his dreams, the LORD tested Joseph's character.
Psalm 105:19 NLT

chapter four

CHOOSE COURAGE

After my humiliating speaking engagement, I had to make a choice. Would I choose courage and move forward into my dreams, or choose fear and remain stuck?

I still remember the moment I made my choice.

It was while flying home from that horrible speaking engagement!

An hour went by on the plane, and I continued to stare blankly at the seat in front of me. An hour and ten minutes went by, and I was still fuming, "I can't believe God put me in front of all those ladies and then humiliated me like that!" An hour and fifteen minutes went by and I was agreeing with the lie the enemy was drilling deeper into my head, "You won't find me speaking at church, any church, ever again."

And then it happened.

I wanted to get my mind on something other than that

humiliating speaking experience running through my head, so I decided I would try to distract myself and read something. But the only reading material I had was my Bible, my sermon notes, and the airplane emergency booklet. I definitely wasn't going to read my sermon notes. No way! And since I had already flipped through the airplane crash booklet at least twenty times, the only other option I had left was my Bible. (I hate being honest here.) I reached into my purse and pulled my Bible out. When I did, it fell open to this passage, and in my amazement here's what I read: *"No servant is greater than his master. If they persecuted me, they will persecute you also." (John 15:30 BSB)*

"Really? I mean, really, God? Can't we find a better promise-verse than this one to meditate on right now?"

I knew I had to make a choice. I could let defeat move me away from my dreams or allow courage to move me toward my dreams. The choice was mine, but first my mindset had to change. God didn't cause this humiliating experience to happen to me. He didn't send those women there to hurt me. He loves them just as much as He loves me. What was I so sad about? Jesus faced more ridicule — much more — than I ever had or ever would!

So why don't I just quit whining and get on with it.

The truth is those women most likely had had something similar happen to them that was now happening to me. My guess is at some point in their lives they had given up on a dream. They no longer believed in the message on faith I preached that night, because the Dream Thief had already stolen their dreams. I mean, honestly, I wasn't that far along on the path of pursuing my dream to become a speaker and writer, so why not avoid some of the pain and just go ahead and give up now?

As tears filled my eyes, I reflected on the beautiful moment I had shared with that one brave woman who had courageously made the decision to make her way down front — in front of all those staring eyes — and pray with me. The invitation had been made for *all* to believe, but only *one chose* to believe. Only one stepped forward to change her life that night.

As I sat on the plane gazing at the verse my Bible had fallen open to, I made up my mind, then and there, when future troubles came my way, I would never ever blame God again. I chose courage that day and made the decision that I would never let the opinions of others keep me from the path God had put in front of me. I chose courage and conquered public opinion that day! I decided it was no longer about my dream needing the approval of others; it was only about receiving God's approval. After all, in the end, His opinion and approval is the only one that counts!

Choose Courage

If we're going to break out of our boxes and reawaken our dreams, then we have to let go of fear and grab hold of courage. Thankfully that's where rage ultimately led me. It led me to courage. You'll need to let rage do the same for you. It's the only way to get from where you are to where you want to be.

But first let's define our terms.

According to Webster, Courage is defined as mental or moral strength to venture, persevere, withstand danger, difficulty or FEAR.

Did you catch that? Courage is needed to withstand fear!

The presence of fear doesn't disqualify us from being courageous. It does the opposite. Fear qualifies us to choose courage and overcome whatever it is we're fearful of! *Just like stars can't shine without darkness, courage can't shine without fear.* We can either conform to our difficult circumstances and let fear control us or we can choose courage and let it lead us. It's a choice, and the choice is ours.

I could have allowed the fear of my cancer to control me. I could have allowed my fear of becoming a speaker or a writer to hold me back. Instead, just like I chose to jump out of that airplane and leave fear behind, I chose courage and moved into the dreams God had given me.

When the door opens, even if it seems as if you're crazy, choose courage and jump! Sure, you'll still feel fear, but that's okay; jump anyway!

Courage is being scared to death and saddling up anyway.
John Wayne

Faith or Courage?

What I started to realize in my own life is that I would often use faith as an excuse to not choose courage. I know that statement sounds strange, but let me explain.

The moment we become a follower of Jesus, faith is given to us as a gift. Paul the Apostle states it this way: *God has allotted to each one of us a measure of faith* (Romans 12:3 NASB). So there you have it. We all have faith. And according to Jesus, it takes only a small amount of faith to accomplish great things. "*Truly I tell you, if you have faith as small as a mustard seed, you can say to this mountain, 'Move from here to there,' and it will move. Nothing will be impossible for you.*" (Matthew 17:20 NIV)

So if you're a follower of Jesus, you already have faith.

I used to confuse my need for more faith with my excuse for not choosing courage. But what I finally realized is that I needed to stop wasting so much time praying for more faith and start praying for more courage. Then and only then could courage activate my faith.

There's a big difference between the two.

Praying for faith keeps us in a place of waiting on God, when in fact He's already deposited everything in us that we need to accomplish *more than all we ask or imagine (Ephesians 3:20 NIV).* What I've found in my own life is the only *one* holding me back from doing more of what God wants to do in me, and what God wants to do through me, is ME. Could it be that you face the same challenge? Could it be that what's holding you back isn't actually a lack of faith but actually a lack of courage?

Courage is a key that opens the door for faith to shine.

When Jesus invited Peter to walk on the water, Jesus didn't offer Peter faith, he offered him *courage.* Jesus specifically said, *"Take courage it is I, do not be afraid." (Matthew 14:27 NIV) Courage* is what got Peter out of the boat, and then *faith* in Jesus is what gave Peter the ability to walk on the water.

Just so I'm clear. I'm not saying we shouldn't pray for faith, or sing about faith, or ask God for more faith. But when the writer of the book of Hebrews says, "*Without faith it is impossible to please God" (Hebrews 11:6 NIV)*, he wasn't addressing something they *didn't have;* he was addressing something they already had but they *weren't using.*

What I learned through my battle with cancer — and I'm still learning — is that it's often not that I need more faith, but more courage. Let me encourage you, actually let me challenge you, find the courage you need to activate your faith so you can become the person God wants you to become and accomplish the things God wants you to accomplish.

It's your choice!

Choose To Fight

But here's the deal; once you choose courage, once you jump and leave fear behind, you'll have to fight.

One night while my kids were still young, I had a dream I was in a severe car accident. I could hear my kids' screams, and then I watched as one by one they were put in an ambulance and rushed away. I awoke in a panic.

The next morning I shared my dream with Ronnie, and we immediately joined hands and prayed. We declared that the enemy had no authority over us. We declared that Satan had no power to harm us. We declared we would not walk in fear.

> *Behold I give you the authority to trample on serpents and scorpions, and over all the power of the enemy, and nothing shall by any means hurt you.*
> ***Luke 10:19 NKJV***

Every day Ronnie and I continued praying over our children. Yet I must admit, I was still fighting fear. I was still tormented by the gruesome dream I had had; the sights, the sounds. But I kept fighting. I refused to let fear overtake me. Instead, I courageously stood on the fact that God had heard our prayers; and no matter what harm the enemy had planned for us, God would keep us.

It was only a week later.

The kids and I were on our way to our church's midweek service, when all of a sudden, BAM! The airbags exploded, and the next thing I knew I was living my nightmare. I looked over at my kids; and even though there was some blood, thankfully, the injuries weren't as severe as what I had seen in my dream.

Four vehicles were involved in the accident. Guess what the car responsible for the accident had plastered all over its back bumper? Numerous stickers declaring she was a witch. Her husband showed up shortly after, and guess what he had splattered all over his bumper and back window? Even more stickers declaring he was a satanic priest!

Now you can call that a coincidence if you want, but I don't think so. I believe the enemy had an evil plot planned for us, but God blocked his plan and protected us.

The thief's purpose is to steal, kill and destroy.
My purpose is to give them a rich and satisfying life.
John 10:10 NLT

I had never been in a car accident with my kids before, nor had I ever had a dream that real before. I just knew God had warned me through my dream that an attack was coming, and He led Ronnie and me to pray over our family. Even though an accident did occur, and we walked away with a few bumps and bruises, there was not *one* broken bone and not one night spent in the hospital. God is so, so faithful.

You meant evil against me
but God meant it for good.
Genesis 50:20 NKJV

Keep Fighting

Maybe you're reading this book, and you've given up on your dreams. People haven't been good to you. Life hasn't been kind to you. You've had experiences that have caused you to stop dreaming. You've settled into autopilot, living a dead-end life. You no longer exude passion. You no longer expect good things to come your way. You no longer believe in living an extraordinary life. You're just going through the motions, holding on to the side of the boat hoping to survive, allowing life to toss you wherever it wants. You've simply lost your will to fight.

But there is a way to regain your will to fight.

First, acknowledge you have an enemy. Second, realize Satan hates you and wants to destroy you. Satan is the source of everything evil and the instigator behind everything that has ever harmed you. Satan is the plotter behind every plan to further harm you.

God certainly isn't the one to put sickness on you or the one to cause bad things to happen to you. God is not against you. God is for you. Yet Satan loves it when we blame God for the sickness or pain or harm that comes our way. Satan loves it when we blame the bad things that happen to us or someone else — a friend, a family member, an authority figure — on anyone but him.

Yes, people may have played a part in discouraging you or harming you. Sure, some people may have been weak enough to allow Satan to use them like a pawn in a plan against you; but ultimately it's the devil. He's the one who uses whom he can and what he can to hurt you, harm you and, if he can, ultimately destroy you.

If he can't destroy you, he at least wants to destroy your dreams. He at least wants to take away your desire to live a purposeful life. And to do so, he works really, really hard to do whatever he can to take away your will to fight. To become passive and be pushed around by his plans.

> *We wrestle not against flesh and blood but against principalities, against powers, against the rulers of the darkness of this world, against spiritual wickedness in high places.*
> ***Ephesians 6:12 KJV***

Simply put, Jesus and the devil both have *plans* for your life and they are starkly different. Satan wants you to either waste your life away or go the whole way and destroy your life. He also wants you to influence those around you to do the same.

Jesus, on the other hand, created you for a purpose, with a purpose. God created you with your own unique *Why* already embedded in your DNA. He doesn't want you to waste your life, and He certainly doesn't want you to destroy your life. He wants you to fulfill the dreams He's placed in your life.

The world needs what God has placed in you. Cures are waiting to be discovered. Books of insight and hope need to be written. Songs of love and joy need to be sung. The seeds are already there.

I love this quote by the late Myles Monroe:

The graveyard is the richest place on the surface of the earth because there you will see the books that were not published, ideas that were not harnessed, songs that were not sung, and drama pieces that were never acted.

Don't stop dreaming. And whatever you do, don't stop fighting. Let your rage lead you to courage, and let your courage lead you into the life God has for you.

Choose Wisely

It's not a matter of choosing courage; it's a matter of what kind of courage and for what purpose will you use the courage you choose. I've seen people do some very evil things. I've also seen very courageous people do some incredibly good things.

So will it be for good, or will it be for evil?

The Bible shows us the importance of not just choosing any kind of courage, but choosing the right kind of courage; choosing **GOOD** courage.

"Wait on the Lord: be of good courage, and he shall strengthen thine heart: wait, I say, on the Lord."
Psalm 27:14 KJV

"Have not I commanded thee? Be strong and of **good** *courage; be not afraid, neither be thou dismayed: for the LORD thy God is with thee whithersoever thou goest."*
Joshua 1:9 KJV

"Be of **good** *courage, and he shall strengthen your heart, all ye that hope in the Lord."*
Psalm 31:24 KJV

Sadly we've all become accustomed to hearing stories of people who do crazy things in the name of courage. Or we hear terms such as 'liquid courage' or 'courage in a bottle,' but that's not real. It's distorted courage and will not lead you to a free life. And let's just be honest... it takes some nerve to do hardcore drugs, to walk out on your kids, or to commit suicide. But that's not what we are talking about. That's again a sick and warped courage that the enemy has distorted. It's rage without the heart. It's twisted and certainly isn't **good** courage. Good courage is fighting through the hard times for your kids and never giving up! Fighting the addiction and doing whatever it takes to keep the faith even in the midst of perilous times. The Bible makes it clear in John 8:44 NIV that the devil is a liar and the father of all lies. If there's anything I will give him a trophy for it's that. A fraud. He has a way of distorting everything to make you believe it's the truth. Remember Eve? *"You will not certainly die." (Genesis 3:4 NIV)* Maybe you are reading this right now and have heard that same deceiving voice whispering in your ear things like, "God doesn't care about you," and "Your family would be so much happier if you weren't around." Those are lies.

That's why we have to be careful to choose the right voice to listen to. I've seen the enemy unable to kill a believer with a physical sickness but then turn around and fight him with a mental illness that leads to suicide.

According to the *American Foundation For Suicide Prevention*, in 2020 suicide was the 10th leading cause of death in the United States.

On average, 132 Americans died by suicide each day.

1.4 million Americans attempted suicide.

I'm not sure about you, but I will no longer be silent and allow the enemy to continue manipulating, confusing, and convincing people, when they are struggling, to take their lives rather than reaching out for help. I will no longer stand on the sidelines doing nothing while Satan stands on the sideline, smiling. Not on my watch!

This may seem too dark for some of you, but again rage always leads us somewhere. The question is, where will you let rage lead you? Will you let rage lead you to courage? Will you let courage give you the will to fight for what God has for you? Or will you settle for the life the enemy is offering you? Which kind of courage will you choose? Will you choose **good** courage and live? The choice is yours.

Let's be honest.

All the enemy knows are lies. His success depends on people believing his lies. It's the Bible who speaks truth, and it's the TRUTH that will set us free. The truth is, someone reading this book needs to wake up and realize the enemy is afraid of you. He wants you dead. If Satan had the power to actually kill you, he would have already done so. The real truth is, God is for you; and if He is for you, who can be against you? No one!

The battle is not against who we have been; it is all out war against who we are becoming.
Lisa Revere

I know this chapter is not for everyone, but I believe it's for someone that was meant to read this. Yes, heaven and hell are both offering courage to you, so choose wisely. Choose **GOOD** courage and LIVE! You may have to fight a lot harder; but remember, you're not fighting alone. Jesus is INSIDE you. He's fighting FOR you. He's fighting WITH you. So regardless of what the enemy throws your way, with confidence you can boldly say, *"Greater is He that is in you (me) than he that is in this world."* (1 John 4:4 KJV)

I want to stop right here and speak to this lying enemy. For far too long he's messed with people's minds, planting thoughts of evil, harm, and destruction. He's continually whispering lies telling you, "You'll never be good enough! Your life is never going to change. Just go ahead and give up." But don't give in to your fears and don't give into his lies.

Let me give you some advice:

Never make a permanent decision due to a temporary problem!

When the economic crash hit Wall Street in 2008, we heard stories of people jumping out of windows, due to the failure of the moment. They chose a distorted courage that couldn't see past their current defeat, rather than courage to believe things could get better — things would get better! They didn't listen to the voice of truth in Jeremiah 29:11 NIV - "For I know the plans I have for you" declares the Lord, "plans to prosper you and not to harm you, plans to give you hope and a future." Now, years later we see that the economy has changed, and it's changed for the better. So the question is: Did people really need to accept defeat?

Let me say it again:

Never make a permanent decision due to a temporary problem!

Don't believe your fears. They will always try to get you to give up. Don't believe his lies. He will always try to stop you. It takes as much courage to believe your fears as it does to trust God by faith! So why not take the same energy it takes to believe your fears and use that energy to trust God by faith.

Whether you're facing a divorce, a sickness, a loss, a financial setback — know that your pain won't last forever. Maybe you directly caused the pain, or maybe you were an innocent bystander. Regardless, every season has an end; and your difficult season will come to an end as well. This may be a bad chapter in your life, but it's not the whole story. Even with a terminal illness the enemy still doesn't win, as the Bible says Jesus conquered death, hell, and the grave! Even in death Jesus still wins, but trust him with all your days. Know that he has your days numbered and don't try to cut them short. *The American Foundation for Suicide Prevention* estimates over 950,000 years of potential life were lost to suicide before age 65. That's a tough statistic to comprehend as we are talking about close to one million years cut short. You don't think out of one million years there would not be some good days?

Ups and downs. Joys and sorrows. Expectations and disappointments. That's the ebb and flow of life. So if you're in a difficult season, if the enemy is trying to take you under, if you've given up on your dreams, if you've lost the will to fight — let me encourage you to keep going.

Choose **GOOD** courage and live.

God loves you. He's for you. He's with you. Believe you're strong enough to fight whatever battle you're facing. Believe that God has a plan for you; a good plan for you; an even greater plan for you.

Choose courage and live!

Suicidal Help

If you are personally struggling with suicidal thoughts, I want you to take courage right now, reach out to someone you trust and tell them what you are going through. The enemy loves it when we fight battles alone, but this is a battle you need help with. Asking for help does not make you weak;

it makes you stronger! If you do not have someone you can confidently confide in, call your doctor or the national suicide prevention hotline at

1-800-273-8255

Mental illness is a real battle, and you do not need to feel shame. There were times when I struggled with confusing and depressing thoughts due to my hormonal imbalance, and the doctors were able to help me through that temporary season.

DO NOT STRUGGLE ALONE! TAKE COURAGE AND LIVE!

PRAYER

Heavenly Father,
Thank you for offering me this gift of courage today. I choose to receive courage for my own life, as well as to use it to encourage others. Help me to continue trusting you with all my days and never listening to the lies of the enemy. I choose to listen to YOUR VOICE and tune out the voice of the enemy. Lord, give me wisdom as I read my Bible and learn the truth of what you created me for. I surrender to you and trust you with all the good, the bad and the ugly.
Love,
Your Encourager from this day on

Quotes to Remember:

Stars can't shine without darkness, and courage cannot shine without fear.

The presence of fear does not disqualify you from being courageous.

Do not conform or agree with fear.

Heaven and hell are both offering courage; choose wisely.

Never make a permanent decision due to a temporary problem!

"Take courage it is I, do not be afraid."
Matt 14:27 NIV

chapter five

HEALING THE RAGE

Over time, the rage boiling inside of me didn't go away; it actually got worse.

Not only did "Momma Bear" come out fighting — at pretty much everything and everyone — but The Incredible Hulk started showing up too. Do you remember The Incredible Hulk, whose anger gave him fuel to fight? At first glance that doesn't seem like a bad thing. We should fight for ourselves, right? But when The Hulk's rage took over, no one was safe — not even innocent bystanders. That's what happened to me. Everyone around me was at risk.

When Momma Bear came out and The Incredible Hulk showed up to help, I felt anger like never before! Up to this point in my life I had also always been a master at containing my emotions, and had never allowed such passionate emotions like anger or rage to have a place in my heart. So when Momma Hulk Bear showed up, I found myself in new territory.

Granted, my anger was targeted toward my battle for my health, which was the right place to aim it; but it was also aimed at everything and everyone else. I was angry at how I had managed over the years to stuff everything down. I was angry at everyone who had done me wrong over the years. I was angry at my friends. I was angry at family members.

And…I was angry at myself.

It wasn't until cancer became part of my story that I realized how many areas of my life I had compromised, not only to appease others, but because I was also afraid of failing. I had always wanted to live my dreams; and even though it was an early cancer diagnosis, it was a wake-up call to reexamine my life. I was angry at just how much time I had wasted living in fear and conforming to the expectations of others. I was so angry that I had put myself into my own little Barbie Doll house. I hated it.

My anger was also directed at my husband. I was angry — really angry — at Ronnie and what our marriage had become. How did we get here?

When I got married (at the age of 17), I was madly, madly in love as most teenagers are. But we were kids! I had a lot of brokenness in my life but just thought, "I'll go ahead and get married and let my Prince Charming fill all my voids and fix all my brokenness. I mean, isn't that what happens in the movies?"

Little did I know that my Prince Charming had his own struggles, and evidently he had watched the same movies I had. So here we were, two needy, broken people who loved each other, but didn't know how to fix one another! And since we couldn't fix one another, we started blaming one another. I said it was his fault. He said it was my fault. I would yell at him, "If you would just get your act together, I could get my act together." He would yell back, "No, if you weren't so needy I wouldn't be so needy." Back and forth we would go.

Of course my anger didn't help. I was angry at the world — and Ronnie was a big part of that world — and since we hadn't dealt with a lot of our issues over the years, we had both settled for the kind of marriage neither one of us really wanted. We were on a downward spiral with a not-so-story-book ending just waiting to happen.

Do You Want To Be Healed?

So here I was, angry at myself, angry at my husband, angry about my marriage, and angry at almost everyone around me.

What was I to do?

Of course I knew the scripture that said, "Be ye angry, and sin not: let not the sun go down upon your wrath." (Ephesians 4:26 KJV) So I knew it was okay to be angry at certain things for a certain span of time. But I also knew that when anger parks in a person's life, that's when a person has a problem. I knew I had a problem.

I took a deep drink of courage and set off on a journey to heal my rage. I wasn't sure where the journey might lead me, but I headed out anyway. It wasn't easy, and it wasn't pretty; but over time I discovered my healing and entered into a life of greater wholeness.

Here's how it happened for me.

RAGE was meant to be a gas station
not a rest area.
If you stay too long you may never leave.

Face It

The first thing I had to do was face it. I had to take ownership of my rage. I knew if I was going to get healed from these passionate and powerful, yet harmful emotions, I was going to have to face them. I had to admit I was holding onto anger, and I wanted to release it. If I didn't, rage would take me down a path I didn't want to go. I decided to stop masking my marriage problems behind anger and needed to be realistic about our situation. It was not an overnight success, but one of the most freeing things I had done was admit everything was not ok. Sometimes deciding who you are is deciding who you'll never be again.

In Genesis 42 we read how Joseph faced it.

His brothers had come to the palace seeking food for their families in the midst of a famine. Their lives were in his hands, yet his brothers didn't even recognize him. I'm sure they assumed he was dead in the well where they left him, or they thought he was at least living as a slave in some foreign land. But here Joseph was, no longer that vulnerable brother they had taken advantage of. He had changed. He was a prince, clothed in strength and power, standing right in front of them.

I find it interesting that Joseph recognized his brothers, but his brothers didn't recognize him. Could it be that Joseph recognized his brothers because they hadn't changed and they didn't recognize him because he had changed so dramatically?

It reminds me of how many people never face their anger, and never find the courage to do so. You cross paths with them years later and they're the same bitter people they were years before. It's heartbreaking. They're still angry at all the wrongs that have been done to them, or angry about all the things they think should have been done for them.

They haven't allowed God to use their pain to change them, to grow them. They haven't allowed God to do His work in them, so He can further do His work through them. They haven't allowed God to use their past to prepare them and promote them into their future. Instead, here they stand, all these years later — bitter, angry, stuck!

> You can never truly defeat something until you have the courage to face it.

What I've learned through my own experiences and observing the lives of others along the way is that, if the enemy can't destroy you with the hurt you've faced, he'll at least try to use the emotional pain left in its wake to deform you. He'll try to keep you caught in your cage of self-pity and shame. He'll try to keep you chained to your past through regret or bitterness. He'll try to keep you from any vision for your future by keeping you locked in your present prison of pain.

God knows these emotions can take us down a destructive path we really don't want to go down, so He graciously warns us to get rid of them. The Bible is clear and pretty emphatic on the remedy and our needed response: "Watch out that no poisonous root of bitterness grows up to trouble you, corrupting many." (Hebrews 12:15, NLT) "For if you forgive others their trespasses [their reckless and willful sins], your heavenly Father will also forgive you." (Matthew 6:14 AMP)

Not only does the Bible warn us of the danger of these destructive emotions, but many studies within the medical community confirm these warnings as well. For example, according to the NCBI - National Center for Biotechnology Information, in the United States, women represent 80 percent of all cases of autoimmune disease. Could it be part of our sickness is because we have been too ashamed to deal with our bitterness, resentment, anger, or rage? Do we cowar down when we need to speak up? Is it possible that by stuffing these destructive emotions down, we're literally making ourselves sick? How many of us women cry when angry because we've held it in for so long? How many discover that anger turned inward is depression?

That's what was happening to me.

But that's not what happened to Joseph.

The Bible says after each encounter with his brothers, Joseph was overcome with emotion. Genesis 43:30 NIV reads, "Joseph was *deeply moved at the sight of his brother* (Benjamin), *Joseph hurried out and looked for a place to weep. He went into his private room and wept there."* I believe it was during these times of deep emotion God was allowing Joseph to face the injustices that had been done to him. Face his resentment. Face his anger. Face his pain.

Forgive

Could it be that Joseph not only faced it, but this was also the time when Joseph decided he would forgive? Would he forgive his brothers for what they had done to him? Would he forgive his brothers for how they had wronged him? Would he forgive his brothers for how they had tried to harm him?

Would he face his anger and then forgive? The choice was Joseph's; it was mine, and it's yours as well.

After I acknowledged and faced my rage, it was then time to forgive. I had to forgive those who had wronged me, those who had abandoned me, those who had taken advantage of me, and those who had spoken ill of me. I had to forgive friends and family, strangers and acquaintances. I had to forgive Ronnie. Most importantly, I had to forgive myself. It's the only solution I have found to retaliation and revenge. The only way I've been able to get past blame and resentment, the only antidote for secret, smoldering feelings of rage from the pain of my past is...Forgiveness. Not until I fully forgave my offenders, one by one, name by name, offense by offense, did I gain my freedom. You know, as soon as I allowed that forgiveness into my heart, something amazing happened. The rage was gone. The anger, resentment, bitterness — vanished. I was lighter and the rage that bubbled in my chest was gone. I felt joy again deep in my soul. Oh, what freedom I felt!

Holding a grudge doesn't make you strong; it makes you bitter.

Forgiving doesn't make you weak; it sets you free.

The same can be true for you.

If you face your pain, face your anger, face your regrets, then you, too, can choose to forgive. You don't have to stay stuck, chained to your past. You don't have to let your present be dominated by your past. You don't have to let bitterness or resentment destroy your future. You can choose the "better" over the "bitter." Don't stay in your prison. Break free of it.

No, it won't be easy. It will take courage. It will take hard work. It will take vulnerability, honesty, and humility. But if you choose good courage, you will experience healing and wholeness like you've never experienced before.

Like Joseph, you, too, can face it, forgive, and find freedom.

Fight

The fight wasn't over for me, though. In addition to facing it and then forgiving, I had one more step to take in my healing journey. I had to use my rage and turn it toward my enemy and fight.

The Bible says, "We wrestle not against flesh and blood but against principalities and powers." (Ephesians 6:12 KJV) It wasn't me, my husband, or anyone else whom I was fighting — or at least shouldn't be fighting. Satan was my rival; he was the target I began fighting!

Together, Ronnie and I decided instead of fighting each other, we would start fighting *for one another*, and in turn fighting for our marriage. God showed us that one of the greatest weapons we had against our enemy was to fight for each other. As Solomon, the wisest man in the Bible, reminds us, "Two are better than one. If either of them falls down, one can help the other up." (Ecclesiastes 4:9-10 NIV) Ronnie and I started warring against our enemy, walking hand in hand. I was stronger with my husband by my side than I ever was on my own.

God had so much more in store for us and our enemy knew it. This is why he fought so strongly against us. So what did we do? We faced our hurts, forgave one another, and started fighting against our enemy.

> A happy marriage is the union of two good forgivers.
> *Ruth Graham*

I then vowed that I would fix my anger on the only one left — the one who comes to kill, steal, and destroy.

Fighting Smart

But there's a warning here.

If you're going to fight, you have to fight smart! It's like when boxers are in training, and they are taught to never lose their temper in the ring. Because if they do, well… they might lose their heads.

The same is true in our fight.

If we're going to fight, we have to fight smart. Yes, we still have to use our rage as fuel to fight our enemy. We still need to stand up and declare war against the evil forces that prey on innocent children. We still need to be angry at the demons who cause cancer and disease. We still need to rage at the enemy who captures millions in his web of addiction and abuse. We still need to rage against the evils and injustices that are all around us — but we have to fight smart. We can't let our enemy use our anger against us. If we do, he'll use our anger to deform us or, worse yet, destroy us.

This almost happened with me and I've seen it happen with others. Don't let it happen to you. Don't be a victim to a difficult circumstance you've gone through, and then become a victim to your emotions left in its wake.

Instead, properly process your emotions of anger, of resentment, of rage, and then let these emotions increase your courage and strengthen your resolve. Let it lift you to a higher level and give you an advantage over your fight with the enemy. Your healing will take prayer and perseverance. It will take wisdom and warfare. It will take other people around you to help you along the way. But if you fight smart, if you use your anger for you and not against yourself or against others, you will take the weapon out of your enemy's hand and put it in your hand.

Above all, be the heroine of your life,
not the victim.
Nora Ephron

A Healing Time In My Life

Even though this was an incredibly messy time in my life, it was also a very healing time for me. The messy season gave me the strength to find the root of my rage and then the courage to face it. Momma Bear made things messy and Barbie didn't look too pretty. The Incredible Hulk came out and threw a few people around (not literally, but you know what I mean). Even with all that mess, this season was very much a needed process of healing for me.

I was healed from much of my deep emotional pain, and taking another step into greater freedom. I moved closer to who I really was in Christ and seeing a bit more clearly who God had called me to become and what God had called me to accomplish. Like I said earlier - *Sometimes deciding who you are is deciding who you'll never be again.*

My journey of healing wasn't over yet.

PRAYER

Heavenly Father,
I'm asking you to give me the courage to face the things I need to change in my life. Help me forgive those who have wronged me and set me free. Give me the strength to boldly confront the hurts I've buried down deep and the wisdom I need to let them go. I know that, with you by my side, I can face everything in my past and everything in my future. I'm ready to move forward, not allowing the past to hold me in my prison any longer. I release all the pain right now into your hands and trust you to bring something beautiful out of it all. Thank you for being the protector of my heart and my loving, faithful friend.
Love,
Your Child

Quotes To Remember:

You can never truly defeat something until you have the courage to face it.

Holding a grudge doesn't make you strong; it makes you bitter.

Forgiving doesn't make you weak; it sets you free.

You are not just a survivor; you are a walking miracle.

You are what you allow.

chapter six

CINDERELLA AND THE INCREDIBLE HULK GET MARRIED

It was during my season of rage that I went with my daughters, Riley and Selah, to see the movie, *Cinderella.* The story is obviously a fairytale; but as I watched Cinderella deal with the cruel mistreatment from her stepmother and stepsisters, I was surprised to discover some tools hidden in the movie for my own healing. I began to see how Cinderella managed to be graceful in the midst of very ugly and unfair treatment. I noticed how Cinderella continued to be kind in a very unkind situation.

I want to tell you a secret that will see you through all the trials that life can offer. Have courage and be kind.
Cinderella

Like Cinderella, one of my greatest challenges during my season of rage was to understand how to navigate these two very different emotions. How can I be angry at the "right" things, yet still be kind? I had gone from being insecure, having too little confidence, and having been run over by too many people to being full of rage, running over everything and everyone in my path. My challenge was to figure out how I could continue to let rage lead me to courage, and let courage lead me to greater wholeness, yet still be graceful and kind. And what a major challenge it proved to be. I've always struggled with setting boundaries and have learned some pretty painful lessons due to that mindset. Empathy without boundaries is dangerous. I knew I had to find the balance.

Courage

In a moment of reflection, I found my answer in an unexpected place — the actual word *courage*.

The root of the word courage is **cor**, which means *heart* in Latin. The second part of the word courage is **rage**. In this one word we have two very passionate and seemingly bipolar ideas. On the one hand is the word *heart,* which is defined as a capacity for sympathy, feeling, and affection. On the other hand is the word *rage,* which Merriam-Webster defines as fury, anger, and outrage. Two *w*ords that come together to create *courage*.

Therefore we do not lose heart.
2 Corinthians 4:16 NIV

The ideas found at the heart of the word courage is a lot like Cinderella and The Incredible Hulk getting married. It's having a passionate heart to fight while keeping a kind heart while we fight. Unfortunately, within much of the feminist movement today we see a lot of this Incredible Hulk kind of rage — without the kindness. Don't get me wrong, I wholeheartedly understand and agree with the need to speak up about certain issues that many women face. I agree that as women we have been silent for far too long. We need to stand up and have our voices heard. We have gone too long standing aside as meek, mild-mannered individuals.

I just can't help wondering about some of the methods being used to show some of the outrage of women. When women march down the streets screaming obscene profanities, while wearing vulgar pictures of vaginas on their heads, is that really going to bring about the change that's needed? It's been my observation that people generally tune out a ranting voice of rage, but will listen to a strong, bold, voice of courage. There are women in other countries who literally have no rights at all, and that is enraging. Baby girls that are abandoned or murdered due to their gender. Girls that are being sold as sex slaves and trafficked while blind eyes just look away. We need to learn how to start movements that can actually invoke change. So there's got to be a better way to share our message, display our courage, *and* keep our dignity.

In the tenuous times we are all currently living in with the covid virus, political unrest, and racial divide, we have all seen social media turn into a place where people are fighting each other more than fighting the real issues. Fighting the problems rather than fighting to find solutions. That's always the enemy's plan—to cause division. Divide and conquer. And when you start believing your Facebook or Twitter friends are your enemies, things can get bad really fast. (I'll repeat this verse again) Ephesians 6:12 NIV says, "*For our struggle* ***is not against flesh and blood,*** *but against the rulers, against the authorities, against the powers of this dark world and against the spiritual forces of evil in the heavenly realms.*" The truth is you are not fighting people; you are fighting a spirit of division, and when you can identify that truth you will start to have real conversations with people of a different opinion rather than attacking each other.

Learning how to stand up to others who wanted to bully me, run over me, or take advantage of me — while keeping my heart kind — was one of my greatest challenges, and honestly still is. It will probably be a challenge for the rest of my life. Yet I knew that figuring out how to remain gracious and kind while demonstrating true courage was critical. I know it was critical, because it's the only way we can demonstrate true courage in a Christ-honoring way.

Admittedly, it isn't easy. But over time, I discovered three keys to being angry yet still being kind.

Finding God In Your Pain

First of all, you have to find God in your pain.

A few weeks after my surgery, while dealing with some very deep and dark physical and emotional pain, I had an encounter with God. I had never before experienced such darkness in my life — never, and, I was really afraid. I was so depressed I couldn't get out of bed. My Bible was the only thing that would give me peace, so I slept with it every night. I remember going to bed that night sobbing, begging God to take me out of this terrible pit.

During the night I had a dream.

I was sitting alone in this dark pit when Jesus suddenly walked up to me. My heart started to race. Jesus was finally coming to rescue me! I lifted my arms like a child, waiting for Jesus to pick me up, but He didn't. Instead, He sat down next to me. I became angry.

"Jesus, why aren't you taking me out of this horrible place?" I started pulling on His arm shouting, "Why are you just sitting here? Please! Take me out of here!" Jesus looked at me and gently said, "Krystal, you will get out of this pit; but right now, you don't have the strength for the journey. Don't worry; until you leave this place, I will be right here by your side." A complete peace came over me; and with tears running down my face, I smiled, laid my head on Jesus' shoulder and fell asleep.

When the enemy brings fear, God brings peace.

I awoke from my dream knowing I had found Jesus in the midst of my pain.

Most of us, however, want to run through our pain, or blame everyone else because of our pain. Yet, no matter what the reason is that we're experiencing pain, or no matter who is responsible for that pain, it's very, very important that we find Jesus in the midst of our pain. When we do, when Jesus comes and heals us, we will experience a new level of compassion and kindness. We will experience grace that softens our hearts. That grace will soon flow from our hearts and into the hearts of others.

There are those reading this book who have faced unfathomable hurts and trauma; and I hope you can hear my heart when I say with the deepest compassion that I am so sorry for what you have been through. Yes, you can be angry. Yes, you can have rage; and Yes, you should seek justice! But allow Jesus to be in your pain with you. Don't allow yourself to stay stuck!

When we find Jesus in our pain, we can still stand for righteousness. We can still stand up for ourselves. We can still fight against injustices and be angry at the things we should be angry about. It's all possible to do with kindness and compassion, with grace and graciousness. As Jesus embraces us and we embrace Him, we can go through the pain without being hardened by it.

Some people are lost in the fire; others are built from it.

It reminds me of the story in the Bible of the three Hebrew children. Daniel describes the story this way: "Lo, I see four men loose, walking in the midst of the fire, and they have no hurt; and the form of the fourth is like the Son of God." (Daniel 3:25 KJV) The three Hebrew children were thrown into the fire, but they weren't harmed. Not only were they not harmed, God was right in the middle of the fire with them.

Again, here's how Daniel recounts the story.

"Then Nebuchadnezzar came near to the mouth of the burning fiery furnace, and spake, and said, 'Shadrach, Meshach, and Abednego, ye servants of the most high God, come forth, and come hither.' Then Shadrach, Meshach, and Abednego, came forth in the midst of the fire. And the princes, governors, and captains, and the king's counsellors, being gathered together, saw these men, upon whose bodies the fire had no power, nor was the hair of their head singed, neither were their coats changed, nor the smell of fire had passed on them."

Daniel 3:26-27 KJV

Wow! Not even any harmful residue left on them.

Now that's amazing, and that's exactly what God wants to do for you. He wants you to find Him right in the midst of your pain. As you do, He'll heal you. And as He heals you, your heart will become more compassionate and more kind. I've never met anyone who went through a season of great suffering and who allowed God to be with them in their pain that, once they came out of the fire, aren't more empathetic, more caring, more compassionate, and more kind.

God went into the pit with Joseph and into the fire with the three Hebrew children, and He'll do the same for you. Embrace God in your pain and let Him embrace you. If you do, He'll use the situation you've gone through to make you better not bitter, to make you stronger not weaker, to make you a victor not a victim. God will come and heal your pain and make you more compassionate and more kind.

First, seek Him in your pain.

Finding Purpose In Your Pain

Second, find purpose in your pain.

God promised He would never leave you nor forsake you, so whatever it is you've gone through, or are going through, God was there with you. He is there with you now! He wants to heal you from what you've gone through, while intentionally using your pain for growth.

When we find purpose in our pain it moves us away from brokenness and bitterness, into meaning and purpose. It moves us away from our self-pity and self-centeredness, and moves us toward the concerns and into the care of others. But the opposite of this is also true. If we don't eventually find purpose in our pain, we will stay in our pain; and if we stay in our pain, our hearts will become hardened.

That's not what God wants for us. God wants to use whatever it is you've gone through to shape you into the image of His Son — and to move you into the destiny He has planned for you.

If you want to express courage in a Christ-honoring way, first find God in your pain and let him soften your heart with greater kindness and compassion. Then find your purpose in your pain and use that purpose to serve others.

Use Our Words Wisely

There's a third way I've learned to be courageous yet kind — and that's by using our words wisely.

The Bible says there is power in our words. Proverbs pointedly puts it this way, "The tongue can bring death or life." (Proverbs 18:21 NLT) That's no small thing.

Courage is a two-way street. We can use our words to put courage in, both within ourselves and within those around us, or we can use our words to take courage out.

I read a story about the first time Joel Osteen took the platform after his father had passed away. He said he was so nervous to step up and take the position as the senior pastor of Lakewood Church, but he did it anyway. After his first sermon, he overheard two women gossiping that he wasn't as good a preacher as his dad.

Wow, talk about words that could have discouraged him at a very inopportune time in his life. Just imagine if he had listened to their words and allowed that to stop him? There would be millions of lives today that would never have been changed. Look at him now. He has one of the most successful ministries in the world, but it all started with a dream and then choosing courage to step into that dream and not allowing what other people said about him to keep him from fulfilling God's purpose throughout his life.

What others say to us has the power to either *put courage in* or *take courage out*. If my skydiving instructor had told me he was terrified every time he jumped, well, I'm pretty sure I would have reconsidered my decision to jump. Yet the opposite was true. His words gave me the confidence and the courage I needed. His words put courage into my decision, and I jumped.

In Latin, *courage* originally meant speaking truth from the heart. Our words are a reflection of the courage that lies in our hearts, and what's in our heart is a reflection of whether we've been healed in our pain or not. So we have to ask ourselves, are we encouraging people in their dreams or discouraging them from their dreams? Are we using our words to bring hope and life or are we using our words to bring discouragement and death? Are we encouraging people to step out of the boat, or encouraging them to stay in the boat?

> Life and death are in the power of the tongue, so choose your words wisely.

What I've also observed over the years, is that the advice we give to others is often directly connected to the advice we give ourselves. If we tend to live in fear and rarely take risks, we, out of our own fears, will tend to discourage others. If we tend to live out of courage and faith, we will tend to motivate others toward a life of greater courage and faith.

I hear people casually giving life-altering advice all the time, "If I were you I would have taken them to court." "If I were in your situation I would have left him a long time ago." "If my child did that, I would throw her out of the house." The Bible warns us that we will be held accountable for how we use our words, so I would encourage you to choose them and use them wisely.

Has God ever placed people around you that he wants you to pour courage into; yet by your words, you end up discouraging them instead of encouraging them? Or have you ever *encouraged* someone to do something they shouldn't have done? Have you ever been responsible for adding to the death of someone's dream? Have you ever been a negative voice that's possibly contributed to the end of a friend's marriage? Have your words encouraged your children toward their dreams or been used in the opposite way?

I know these are pointed questions, and believe me they challenge me just as much as you. I hope these questions challenge you because it's important that we honestly evaluate how we use our words. Are we using our words for life or for death? To put courage in or to take courage out? To build people up or to tear people down? Are the words we use based in love or out of our own fears?

Unfortunately, too often we minimize the power of our words and the advice we so easily give to others. If you're a dream killer, let that demonic pattern cease from your mouth. The next time someone approaches you for advice, please take the time to seek God before you casually let words spill out of your mouth. Remind yourself of the weight of your words and what the Psalmist warned about our words: "May these words of my mouth and this meditation of my heart be pleasing to you, O Lord, my Rock and my Redeemer." (Psalm 19:14 NIV) Make a renewed decision today: do not be a dream killer, but a dream encourager.

If we are going to direct our anger in the right direction, if we are going to express courage in the things we need to show courage for — yet still be kind — we need to use our words wisely.

The Right Side Of Discouragement

Believe it or not, using our words for discouragement isn't always wrong. In fact,

We can, and we should, use our words in a way that discourages our enemy. There are many examples of this found in the Bible. One of them is in the book of Joshua: "Now when all the Amorite kings west of the Jordan and all the Canaanite kings along the coast heard how the Lord had dried up the Jordan before the Israelites until they crossed over, their hearts melted in fear and they no longer had the courage to face the Israelites."
Joshua 5:1 NIV

Wow, what a powerful idea.

God used His victories as a weapon to discourage our enemy. This scripture truly excites me because of the potential I, myself, have to discourage the devil. I've allowed the enemy to discourage me more than I would like to admit it. And, regrettably, many times I did the job for him.

But times have changed, my friends. There's a new sheriff in town. I've chosen to make it my lifetime goal to annoy the living hell out of the enemy's camp. Now that I more fully understand the power God has put within me, I've made the decision to use that power and the power of my words against the enemy.

Now, don't get me wrong.

The reality is our circumstances may look worse before they get better. And make no mistake about it, our enemy will do everything he can to intimidate us. But we must remind ourselves that the enemy has no power over us. In fact, the only power he has is the power we give him. And the number one way he tries to gain that power over us, is through what I call his DIS-strategy. He will do anything he can to DIS-courage, DIS-tract, and then DIS-card us.

When we're in a storm the enemy will roar like a lion and try to intimidate us. The Bible describes his actions as "prowling around like a roaring lion seeking whom he may devour." (I Peter 5:8) Notice: he roars *like* a lion but he isn't one. He's only imitating a lion.

There's only one lion, and He's the *Lion of the Tribe of Judah*. He's the One we must stay focused on during our storms. He's the one who rules over all things. He's the one who says, "be healed;" and we're healed. He's the one who says, "be free" and we're set free. He's the only One with all power and authority, and He's already deposited His power and authority in us.

> You've always had the power my dear;
> you just had to learn it for yourself.
> *The Wizard of Oz*

All other voices, except God's voice, are just noises sent by the enemy to distract you, to scare you, to discourage you. He'll do anything he can to get you to back up or back down. Satan knows that if he can just keep you cowered down your whole life, he wins. He knows if he can intimidate you, then you'll *never* choose the courage you need to accomplish the greatness that's already inside of you.

Don't allow him to win! Don't allow his words, or the words

of others, to discourage you. Instead, use your words of courage to discourage him.

Now's the time to wipe away your tears, to choose courage, and walk into the impossible. Now's the time to dream again! Even if you're afraid to start that business you've always wanted to, start it anyway. Even if it seems that the college you want to attend is out of reach, apply for it anyway. Even if your diagnosis seems grim, speak healing over your life anyway.

Don't allow the roar of the enemy to intimidate you. Rise above it! Stop focusing on how many "Nos" you've received, when you need only one "Yes!" Keep your eyes focused on the Lion of the Tribe of Judah. Keep your ears tuned to what God has said to you and what God has said about you! Use your words to speak life, to speak health, to speak wholeness.

I'm praying you'll grab hold of this truth for your life. I pray you'll no longer use discouragement on yourself or those around you. Instead, you'll turn your words around and use them as a way to discourage your enemy. Take all that built up frustration you have, along with your rage for the injustices he's done to you, and literally take the courage out of that thug's camp. Choose today to stop discouraging others and instead start discouraging the enemy.

> *"Don't ever be afraid or discouraged, Be strong and courageous, for the Lord is going to do this to all your enemies."*
>
> ***Joshua 10:25 NIV***

So it's time to confuse your enemy. Properly deal with your emotions of anger, or rage, or resentment. No longer allow your emotions to control you. No longer be vulnerable to the enemy's schemes against you. You will go through the fire and emerge without the smell of smoke on you. You will go through any storm and still smile throughout the night. You will go through abuse and not become its victim. You will fight cancer and not become its perpetual patient. You will do all of this if you control the emotions and make them work with you and for you.

Yes, these battles will change you. Yes, you will look different after you go through them. And yes, there is a way to be courageous and still be kind. So open the door and let Jesus walk with you through the fire. Invite Him into your pit. Welcome him into your prison. He'll gladly show up!

My story isn't over and neither is yours.

You'll never, ever guess what happens next for me.

Prayer

Heavenly Father,
I am asking you to give me the courage to face the things I need to change in my life. Help me forgive those who have wronged me and set me free. Thank you for giving me the strength to boldly confront the hurts I have buried down deep and the wisdom on how to let them go. I know with you by my side I can face everything in my past and my future. I am ready to move forward and no longer allow the past to affect me . I release all the pain right now into your hands and trust you will bring something beautiful out of it. I love you, my faithful friend and protector of my heart.
Love,
Your Child

Quotes to Remember:

Have courage and be kind.

When the enemy brings fear,
God brings peace.

Some people are lost in the fire;
others are built from it.

Life and death is in the power
of the tongue.

Don't ever be afraid or discouraged, Be
strong and courageous, for the Lord is
going to do this to all your enemies.
Joshua 10:25 NIV

chapter seven

TWO LITTLE MIRACLES

It was six weeks after my hysterectomy, and I had just learned that my cancer concerns weren't all cleared. I was waiting for my next appointment with the oncologist at the Orlando Cancer Center to have more biopsies and find out what treatments would be available to me. I was really struggling. I felt like a sitting duck.

I was so depressed I didn't want to get out of bed. Ronnie was trying to help me break my downward spiral, so one morning he came in and said, "Hey Krystal, I've got to do some work on the building at the church; how about getting out of bed and coming down with me? Just come and hang out with me a bit." I really didn't want to, as feeling sorry for myself sounded like a better plan for the day; and with a few short words, I told him so. Ronnie persisted, "Come on. It would really help me out and I'd love for us to be together today." I reluctantly gave in, got dressed and headed to the church.

Little did I know what awaited me.

Ronnie was laying tile in the entryway of our church building, and I was there just keeping him company. Our church was located in a rougher area of town; and as a way to serve our community, three nights a week we offered clothing, toiletries, and hot meals to hundreds of people through our food and clothing ministry. Even though we didn't know everyone's story who came through our outreach ministry, you could visibly see the discouragement and brokenness on their faces. Each person who came through here walked a difficult path, and we tried our best to help them in small ways.

On this particular day, we didn't have an evening outreach planned, yet people from the neighborhood were hanging around outside our building. We were located in a shopping plaza and people seeking shelter would often stay under the awnings during the day, which meant people hanging around outside wasn't uncommon.

On this day, events that were quite different developed.

More than once, Ronnie and I noticed two little boys in diapers who were with a younger couple hanging outside of our church. We assumed the couple were the parents; and they appeared to be half passed out on the sidewalk, concerning both Ronnie and myself. The drug that was popular in our part of Florida was a drug called spice, or the "zombie drug" – so called because of the way it almost instantly reduces users to a semi-comatose state. It was a really common drug in our county, and we were accustomed to seeing the effects on people. Now, we didn't know for sure if that was the drug this couple was on, but it definitely appeared that way.

One of the boys was a toddler — one, or two years old — and he was running around unattended in the church parking lot. The second child had been strapped in a car seat the entire day and was an infant, but old enough to hold his own bottle. Ronnie has always been the "paranoid parent" of the two of us; and with those natural instincts of a worst-case scenario mindset, he was a nervous wreck watching the parents sleep with their toddler running around near the street. Ronnie went out several times, concerned that the toddler was going to run into the six-lane road. Three lanes going in each direction... and it was busy. Every time Ronnie went out, he asked the parents if they needed help. "Hey guys, do you need me to take you anywhere?" They told him, "No, we're fine. We have a tent in the woods nearby and eventually we'll make our way back there." It was apparent they were under the influence of something, and it would be a while before that journey would take place, if ever. As Ronnie and I talked about the situation, we both realized we had seen this couple before. We remembered seeing them sleeping behind the dumpsters at 7-Eleven, and one time at Burger King with a stroller. We never realized there were actual children in the stroller though. We assumed it was a way to travel with their belongings.

Our church had connections with some local agencies that offered housing; and since we had heard a storm was coming our way, Ronnie went back out and offered them assistance with shelter for the night. "Hey guys, I know we can get you a room tonight across the street; do you want me to call over there and set it up?" They nonchalantly declined. We gave them food and urged them to reconsider, but they said they would make it just fine. We wanted to do more but didn't know what more we could do.

Throughout the day the two little boys remained outside our church. The oldest one would come up to the doors, smash his lips against the window and blow his cheeks out as he watched us work. He didn't have any toys to play with so I brought out a matchbox car from the church nursery. You should have seen his big, blue eyes light up. You would have thought it was Christmas! He sat down on the sidewalk and played with that car the rest of the day.

These two precious little boys, whom we later found out were only a year and a half and five months old, were surrounded by deplorable circumstances that were no fault of their own. Ronnie and I would smile and wave at this sweet boy when he came up to the church doors, while inwardly our hearts were breaking.

It was beginning to get dark, and we knew our three kids who had stayed home that day were getting hungry, as we had already been gone longer than we said. So we packed up the flooring materials and locked up the church; and as we were walking to our car, we passed this couple again. Ronnie blurted out over the noise, "You guys sure you don't need anything tonight?" The boys' parents were with a group of people who were hanging out under the nearby awnings as all the businesses had closed, and it appeared they were getting ready for a long night of partying. It was getting pretty rowdy as alcohol and other drugs had now joined the party, and it seemed as if many of them were already pretty "wasted." Right in the middle of that chaos were those two little boys. Ronnie started the car but sat in silence. He didn't put the car in drive; he just sat there staring off in the distance. He didn't have to say anything. I knew what he was thinking as I was thinking the same thing; and as protective parents to our children, we couldn't imagine our kids here in this unsafe situation. We were both struggling at the thought of these boys making it through the night as it seemed impossible they would not be harmed.

I broke the silence, took the deepest breath of courage I could take, looked over at Ronnie and asked, "Honey, since the parents are already high and have refused to go to a shelter for the night, can we just ask them if they want us to take the boys home with us? Just for the night?" I knew Ronnie was thinking the same thing, but it still sounded crazy to say aloud. He looked at me wide eyed and asked, "Are we really sure about this?" With conviction, I responded, "We at least have to try."

Ronnie nodded, got out of the car, and approached the couple. The next words I heard from him were, "Ummm, they said yes."

Without hesitation the mom put an old, blue adult sized polo shirt they'd gotten from our church's clothing ministry on the toddler and then handed me the baby, wearing only a diaper and still strapped in the car seat. She handed me an old bottle that had a brown substance in it and said, "Just mix the formula with baby cereal in the morning and he will drink it throughout the day! Thanks guys, see you tomorrow!"

As we drove away the rain began to fall, and so did my tears. I gazed in the rearview mirror still speechless of the situation unfolding around us. On the one hand I felt humbled that God would allow me to be a part of these two little lives, even if just for the night. On the other hand, I deeply questioned God's wisdom in it all. Had He forgotten I was right in the middle of my own storm? What was God thinking? Why me? Why now? Why couldn't this have happened three months ago when I was stronger?

I silently prayed, "Lord, this mission is way too important for me to mess it up; please give me the strength." I wiped my tears, smiled at the two little miracles sitting in the back seat and told Ronnie we needed to go straight to Walmart, as the aroma that filled our car made it clear a diaper change was long overdue. As we walked the aisles with these two boys, the question in the back of my mind was growing stronger: Where was all of this taking us?

We grabbed a box of diapers, wipes, and Teenage Mutant Ninja Turtle pajamas for the toddler and Cookie Monster pajamas for the baby and headed back to the car to go home.

Good waiters don't just sit around;
good waiters SERVE!

That first night was like a foggy dream. When Ronnie and I came home carrying two babies, our own children had as many questions as we did. "What's going on?" "How did this happen?" "What do we do now?" "What's going to happen next?" The two little boys certainly didn't know what was going to happen next, so they just sat there staring at us with their big ol' eyes!

With so much to do, we pushed our questions aside. We bathed the boys, fed them dinner, and gave them lots of snuggles and hugs.

It wasn't long before we heard the toddler giggling as our daughter Selah was blowing bubbles in the living room, and he thought it was hilarious! His giggle was so loud and deep it made us all laugh so hard, and we kept telling Selah to "do it again!"

After an hour of this bubble fiasco we were all laughed out, worn out, and ready for bed. Ronnie brought a mattress into our room and placed it on the floor next to his side of the bed for the toddler to sleep on. I set up the playpen we brought from the church on my side for the baby to sleep in. We laid them down wondering how this was going to go; and within minutes, they were sound asleep. They were comfortable and they were safe.

I will admit I am crying like a baby right now while remembering this moment as it was so surreal, and we were just so thankful these boys were safe. Ronnie and I joined hands in bed and prayed blessings over them as we did every night over our kids — Ronnie III, Riley and Selah.

Ronnie and I were so tired, but that night we couldn't fall asleep. All we could do was stare at these two little miracles sleeping next to us. Their backstory was somewhat of a mystery to us, but the marks on the toddler's feet told us more than we wanted to know. It looked as though his shoes had been on his feet for weeks. When we took them off to give him a bath, since the shoes were two sizes too small and he didn't have any socks on, the skin from the top of his foot came right off. And the odor...well, it was unbearable. It took everything within me not to break down and cry in front of him. I just couldn't fathom the difficult journey this little boy had already been on in his short life, but his feet told us a lot.

Our lingering questions returned: "Where is all of this taking us?" "What's going to happen next?" We didn't know the answers, but we did know we would need to trust God. He was the only One who knew what was next. We would just have to wait and see.

Waiting In The In-Between

I remember penning these words in my journal reflecting what I felt in this season:

> In the middle...
> I am so far from the shoreline but still can't see the end.
> Will this ever end?
> Can I make it through? Or will my doubt cave in.
> I look to You on high, You have always been my guide.
> Please give me strength to go, when everything in me is saying, WHOA!
> I can't go back now, Your Word says I CAN somehow?
> Can go, can do, can see, can be? Only You know me...
> So with this oar I will ROAR! You promised that with You I can soar.
> So regardless of the tears I pour,
> I will make it to the other shore...

When we're in the middle of a storm, that's when our faith is tested the most. In the middle, waiting to see if the outcome will be what God says or what the doctor says. In the middle, waiting to see if our marriage will survive or cave in. In the middle, waiting to see if a wayward child will return to the narrow path or continue down the broad road leading to destruction. In between what is and what will be, waiting to see what God will do.

What do we do when we're waiting on God? What do we do when we're in a season of in-between?

Many times we do nothing. We assume that, until we know the outcome, our best choice is to do nothing. We're tempted to sit. To wait. To throw up a few faint prayers and hope for the best. But that's not the route the Bible encourages us to go. The Bible tells us that faith without works is dead, so why play dead while we're waiting. Instead, why not exercise our faith? Why not do something? Why not do what God's Word says?

I'm reminded of the story in the Bible where a widow and her son are living in a famine, on the verge of starvation; and God sent the prophet, Elijah. When Elijah arrived, he asked the widow to use the last bit of food she had to make him a meal. That's how I felt. Got was asking me to use the last little strength I had left to care for these two little boys.

The Message, in I Kings 17:8-24, describes this marvelous and miraculous story this way:

Eventually the brook dried up because of the drought. Then God spoke to him: 'Get up and go to Zarephath in Sidon and live there. I've instructed a woman who lives there, a widow, to feed you.' So he got up and went to Zarephath.

As he came to the entrance of the village he met a woman, a widow, gathering firewood. He asked her, 'Please, would you bring me a little water in a jug? I need a drink.' As she went to get it, he called out, 'And while you're at it, would you bring me something to eat?'

She said, 'I swear, as surely as your God lives, I don't have so much as a biscuit. I have a handful of flour in a jar and a little oil in a bottle; you found me scratching together just enough firewood to make a last meal for my son and me. After we eat it, we'll die.' Elijah said to her, 'Don't worry about a thing. Go ahead and do what you've said. But first make a small biscuit for me and bring it back here. Then go ahead and make a meal from what's left for you and your son.

This is the word of the God of Israel: 'The jar of flour will not run out and the bottle of oil will not become empty before God sends rain on the land and ends this drought.' And she went right off and did it, did just as Elijah asked. And it turned out as he said—daily food for her and her family. The jar of meal didn't run out and the bottle of oil didn't become empty: God's promise fulfilled to the letter, exactly as Elijah had delivered it!

Later on the woman's son became sick. The sickness took a

turn for the worse — and then he stopped breathing. The woman said to Elijah, 'Why did you ever show up here in the first place — a holy man barging in, exposing my sins, and killing my son?'

Elijah said, 'Hand me your son.'

He then took him from her bosom, carried him up to the loft where he was staying, and laid him on his bed. Then he prayed, 'O God, my God, why have you brought this terrible thing on this widow who has opened her home to me? Why have you killed her son?' Three times he stretched himself out full-length on the boy, praying with all his might, 'God, my God, put breath back into this boy's body!' God listened to Elijah's prayer and put breath back into his body — he was alive! Elijah picked the boy up, carried him downstairs from the loft, and gave him to his mother. 'Here's your son,' said Elijah, 'alive!' The woman said to Elijah, 'I see it all now — you are a holy man. When you speak, God speaks — a true word!'

Please notice that the widow was in-between. Would she starve or would she survive? Would the meal she makes Elijah deplete her of all she has left, or would it launch the miracle she so desperately needed? Her miracle didn't happen by waiting around. God asked her to do something. He asked her to serve. He asked her to give what she had.

The same is true for you and me.

God never asks us for more than we can give. He already knows how much we have left. Like the widow, when God asks us, if we're willing to give all we have left, that's when our faith is tested. Will He really come through? Can I really trust Him in this?

It's important, however, to understand that the widow didn't do something for God so she could get something from God. That's not how God works. She simply obeyed; and through her obedience, God gave her more than she could ever imagine. She got her son back. She got her life back.

My story is similar.

I would have never imagined that God would choose the most chaotic time in my life to bring these two little boys, these two little miracles, into my life. I felt so weak. I felt so unqualified. Didn't they deserve better than what I could provide? Did God really know what He was doing?

I now understand why God had given me the word "Grace" for this particular season of my life. He knew that His strength, provided by His grace, would be what I would need during the time of my greatest weakness. I could identify with the Apostle Paul when he wrote, "God's grace is sufficient for me, His power is made perfect in my weakness. For when I am weak, then I am strong." (2 Corinthians 12:9,11)

Times of greatest weakness are made for God's greatest miracles. It was that way for me; I know it can be the same for you.

I have great news; another major miracle was still in the making.

If He did it for me, He'll do it for you.

Foster Care / Adoption statistics

According to Children's Rights (childrensrights.org), on any given day, there are nearly 424,000 children in foster care in the United States. In 2019, over 672,000 children spent time in U.S. foster care. On average, children remain in state care for over a year and a half, and five percent of children in foster care have languished there for five or more years.

Of the 400,000 children in foster care, approximately *120,000 are waiting to be adopted.*

PRAYER

Heavenly Father,

I trust you have a plan for my life. Although it's not always clear, I choose to trust you when I'm in the middle of the storm. I will not listen to my doubts, but will focus on you - the way, the truth, the life. I thank you that I'm strong enough to accomplish the mission you have for me in this season. From this day on I'm choosing to not question your timing but to obey when you speak. I know I may be in a season of in-between, but I can't wait to see what you have for me next!

Love,

Your Servant

Quotes to Remember:

Rage dear heart, yet stay kind.

People who make excuses
trarely make a difference.

Good waiters don't just sit around;
good waiters SERVE!

chapter eight

ANOTHER MIRACLE IN THE MAKING

As hard as it was, we did what we promised.

We brought the boys back to the church the next day and dropped them off to their parents, right back into that horrible living situation. Let me make it clear. It wasn't living in the tent that made this such a horrible situation; it was the drugs and neglect. Sadly, in Florida, living in a tent with children is not unheard of as many families, due to various reasons, fall into hard times and end up homeless or living in their cars. Not everyone in these situations are on drugs or chose this life as people are so quick to assume.

Surprisingly, these kinds of living situations are more common than you might think — yes, even right here in the good old United States of America. It's certainly happening in your state and, most likely, right in your very own city. According to The *U.S. Department of Housing and Urban Development*'s 2020 report, it shows there are 13.2 homeless people for every 10,000 residents in Florida, ranking the Sunshine State No. 15 among U.S. states with the largest homeless populations.

Here's a closer look at the findings for Florida in 2020:

Total homeless population: 28,328

Homeless individuals (not in families with children): 21,265

Homeless population in families with children: 7,063

Percentage of homeless population living unsheltered: 44.0%

Percentage of homeless population chronically homeless: 20.2%

Up until that day, I just didn't have the eyes to see what was going on right in front of me. But now I did. Because of the pain happening in my own life, I was able to more quickly recognize the pain in other peoples' lives. And now that I had seen it, I couldn't un-see it. Love chooses to see what others overlook; or another way I've heard it said is, "Love looks around."

I wish I could put into words the hopelessness I felt when we dropped these two

little precious boys off to their parents. Our children were heartbroken as well. They kept

pleading with us, "Please don't take them back. We want them to stay with us. Please can't you let them stay?"

Even though this was a heartrending situation, We gathered as a family and prayed over the boys, asking God to protect them. We dropped them off, gave the parents our phone number, and told them to call if they needed anything!

Then, with great sadness, we said our goodbyes.

Later that night our phone rang.

Ronnie answered. I could tell by the look on his face that something was up. It was the boys' parents. Ronnie looked at me. I looked at him. Ronnie wanted to see what my response was going to be, so he started repeating what the parents were saying. "You want us to meet you at the church and bring the boys back to our home for the night?" I nodded. Ronnie answered, "We'll meet you in twenty minutes."

I was thankful the boys were coming back to be with us for another night, but I wasn't sure how I was going to find the strength.

Somehow, by God's grace, I stumbled forward.

We picked the boys up, and they spent the night with us. As if on repeat, we dropped them back off the next day; and again their parents called and asked if we would take them for another night. And off to Walmart we would go to buy more clothes. This cycle went on for days. I just didn't know how long we could carry on like this, but Ronnie and I trusted in God's plan.

Then the unexpected happened.

It was a Sunday and our church service had just ended. We were walking to our car discussing our plans for lunch, when the boys' mother, along with a social worker, approached us. The mom asked if we would keep the boys while she and her boyfriend were going to try and get some things in their life in order.

I'll never forget the moment.

Here Ronnie and I were, along with our three children, literally standing in the middle of our church's parking lot, making this potentially life-altering decision. Would we sign this handwritten paper giving us limited rights to these two little boys? What would happen to them if we didn't? What would happen *to us* if we did?

The social worker had already told us she was either putting them in her car and placing them in foster care or putting them in our car for our care under the mother's wishes.

We made the decision quickly, but we didn't make it lightly. It was reassuring that the prayers we had prayed as a family, only a few days earlier, were already being answered; but the decision still wasn't easy. We knew this decision could alter the trajectory of our lives, and the future of these two little boys as well. And, honestly, we didn't have any guarantee which direction that trajectory might end up going. The outcome could be quite different from what our hearts wanted.

But we didn't let that stop us.

We decided to let go of fear, grab hold of courage, trust God, and see where this journey would take us.

Courage is like a muscle.
We strengthen it with use.
Ruth Gordon

We signed the papers on the hood of our car. The social worker notarized it. It was a done deal. The mom handed us the boys. I looked at Ronnie, and Ronnie looked at me. We both looked at our three children, Ronnie III, Riley, and Selah as they were smiling.

And guess what we said next? Let's go back to Walmart!

The next five months seemed to fly by, and we were so grateful people in our church stepped up to help by bringing us boxes of diapers, clothes, and meals for our family. The social worker we had met even stopped by our home to drop off a new double stroller and car seats. It was definitely a team effort!

We didn't know what tomorrow might hold, so we attempted to live each day the best we could. In the meantime, Ronnie made it his mission to do everything he could to help the boys' parents; and as a Mister Fix-It, he took them to get new social security cards, haircuts, bought new clothes and drove them wherever they asked in hopes it was all going to lead to a restored life. Unfortunately things were not getting better with their lives and only seemed to be getting worse. They stopped coming around as much, and we were becoming discouraged that our efforts were failing.

On top of this new responsibility with caring for these two little miracles, I was still uncertain of my own future. My appointment with the oncologist to review the biopsies they had taken a few weeks earlier was coming up. I wasn't sure what to expect.

Thankfully, I was regaining some of my physical strength, but still couldn't help wondering how God was going to work all this out.

Was my cancer back? Was I going to be okay? Would I need further treatments?

I sometimes wonder, if I hadn't chosen courage in the small things leading up to this huge challenge I was now facing, would I have had the strength to choose courage in this season? It hadn't been an easy road, and the journey wasn't over; but I was thankful I had continued to trust God all along the way. You see, I believe courage is contagious. It's a snowball effect. Choosing courage to face cancer, public opinion, religious spirits and my marriage problems was the same courage I chose to keep stepping day by day in this crazy season. And as I explained earlier, it's not a feeling; it's an action. Even when you're doing it afraid, you just have to keep walking.

I arrived at the Orlando Health Cancer Institute and was directed to the Gynecologic Center waiting room. As I was signing in and set the pen down, the strangest feeling washed over me as I saw my name on that list. What was I doing here? And then I saw the names above me and thought the same thing... What are any of us doing here? I felt so angry at the word 'cancer' and the fear attached to it and just wanted to scream to everyone waiting, "We don't belong here!"

The nurse called my name, "Krystal Stewart, please follow me;" and there we went down the hallway, past the Infusion Area (aka The Chemo Room). I glanced in the window as I was walking by and saw the most beautiful, courageous women sitting in the recliners receiving treatment. I didn't know any of their stories but I couldn't help wondering what this first day was like for them. In a strange way seeing them gave me courage. I continued following the nurse into the procedure room, and she handed me a paper gown. She was arranging the surgical tools on the tray as she explained what to expect and told me to undress from the waist down as my doctor would be in soon for the biopsies.

She closed the door, and I immediately burst into tears and told Ronnie I was afraid. (I wish I could tell you I was being super positive that day, but I was a blubbering baby, and dramatic…) He tried to reassure me, but my sarcastic comments just started rolling out one by one. "Oh, great! Not only is this room fifty degrees but I now get to wear a piece of paper for clothing!" By the way, can I just comment on this and wonder why, in the twentieth century, are we still wearing paper gowns? Like, seriously? And why do doctors choose to have such vulnerable, life-changing conversations with you while you're half naked with a paper blanket. Ugh.. Ok, moving on... Five minutes later the oncologist came in and re-explained the procedure I would be having. She showed me on my surgical report where it stated I didn't have clear margins and would need to biopsy two different areas. I just wanted to get it over with. I laid back, feet in the stirrups and stared at the ceiling…. She told me she was going to be checking for tumors and then applying a solution that would reveal the areas she needed to biopsy, and it may be uncomfortable. Not to continue ranting but that is code for "it's going to hurt *a lot,*" and with it being applied on my internal incisions it sure did—it felt like fire! I couldn't see what was going on; but a few more minutes passed and she apologized, saying, "I know it's uncomfortable but I need to apply more solution."

I didn't even respond as my legs were visibly shaking by this point; and I was just trying to stay still so this could be done! She told me it was now time for the biopsies; and I would be feeling a few, sharp pinches (can you hear my sarcasm?). I braced for the pain and nothing happened. I kept waiting for the pinch and it didn't come! My doctor sat back and said, "Mrs. Stewart, you can sit up now." I took my feet out of the stirrups, grabbed the paper sheet to cover myself and wondered, "*What now?*" To my amazement her next words were, "Mrs. Stewart, I am not sure what happened, but I did not feel any tumors, and the solution did not reveal any abnormal cells to biopsy as your surgical report indicated." I looked over at Ronnie and back at my doctor and said, "So what do we do now?" She said the best words I have ever heard… "You can go home! I will need to verify this report again in three months, but for now you are done!" I was so elated I was up, dressed, and out of that building as fast as possible! It was a miracle! My surgical report three months earlier that read I needed "further treatment," was wrong and my newest report stated,

"There are NO cancerous areas to biopsy or treat!"
I was elated!
A miracle!

Now, maybe you're thinking that the original report was just a mistake; but I know the truth. God had healed me! No more cancer!

When I heard those joyous words, I was immediately reminded of an old hymn I used to sing as a little girl… *His eye is on the sparrow and I know he watches me.*

With my battle with cancer behind me, I turned my attention to my next area of uncertainty. What would happen to these two little boys? Could one of our days together end up being our last one?

Early on we had made the decision to open our hearts to these boys as if they were our very own family. And we had. In fact, our three children — Ronnie III, Riley, and Selah — were already introducing them to their friends as their little brothers. I knew our hearts were forever changed. We would always be connected to the boys, Dallas and Grayson, as we had a special bond after going through so much together, so I didn't discourage our children from calling them family. We all loved the boys and wanted them to feel as if our home was their home, even if it was only temporary.

Ronnie and I were not foster parents and had only power of attorney, which had previously been signed over to us by the boys' mother. This made the situation tenuous because the State could remove Dallas and Grayson at any time according to their own discretion. No one knew what might happen next. We knew only that we would need to continue trusting in God with whatever his next plan for us was.

Some very alarming news reached us a few months later.

The boys' mother was pregnant again; and since there hadn't been any change in her lifestyle, it was very likely her baby would be taken — straight from the hospital — and placed into foster care. Because we didn't have permanent custody of Dallas and Grayson, it also meant they might be removed from our home and put into foster care as well.

What made this news even more alarming was the mom was already in her seventh month of pregnancy. We had no idea what was going to happen.

It was the boys' mom who broke the news to us of this unfolding situation, and we were shocked! Next she said something I couldn't believe I was hearing, "I've decided I want you guys to adopt the boys. I don't want them in foster care; they have been living with your family for six months, and I can tell they are happy." She continued on and told us she also wanted to make an adoption plan for the baby girl she was pregnant with and asked if we could help.

We were humbled to say the least as this was overwhelming on so many levels and greater than anything we ever imagined. But we were also heartbroken, as it was clear our original hope of their family being restored was not going to happen. We had some *really*, long, painful conversations that day with the boys' mother and learned the father had over ten children with different women and was not able to care for any of them. We were stunned.

As easy as it is for people to judge her, I've always had real love and compassion for her. She and I had *many* private conversations where she shared her desire for her children to grow up in a healthy environment, and she didn't feel she could ever offer that for reasons *I will keep private.* I was inspired by her courageous, yet painful, decision to place her children for adoption. I know it wasn't easy, but she made the decision out of love. *(I will also keep private the details of the adoption plan she made for her daughter as it is not my story to tell, but another beautiful miracle.)*

We told her *of course, it would be our honor and promised to love and raise them as our own.* And then none of us knew what to do next... I called my friend who worked at a Christian adoption agency to ask what we needed to do. She was also shocked by the situation and said *she had no idea,* but gave us the phone number for a private attorney to get some advice. We already knew that time was working against us. The attorney said she could help us with the adoption, but then she dropped another bombshell. With this being a very complex and private adoption, it was going to cost us a lot of money — money we didn't have.

We had already overcome one major battle and defeated cancer, but now we were facing another Goliath. We were once again over our heads with stress and emotional toil. We went ahead, summoned up our courage and signed the contract with the attorney. In faith, we told the attorney, "When the time comes, we'll have the money." At the moment that wasn't anywhere close to reality.

We needed another miracle, so we did what we do best and trusted God. God always works the best in impossible situations (remember the backpack story?).

> *For nothing is impossible to God!*
> ***Luke 1:37 CEV***

Due to my medical bills, our savings account was drained. We had also made several adjustments to accommodate the financial needs of adding the boys, Dallas and Grayson, to our family. And to make this Goliath stand even taller, the kind of adoption we were looking at was so odd and unheard of that we didn't fit into the category to receive any state funding.

What were we to do?

I was well aware of this wonderful promise in God's word: *Now to Him who is able to [carry out His purpose] and do superabundantly more than all that we dare ask or think [infinitely beyond our greatest prayers, hopes, or dreams], according to His power that is at work within us.* (Ephesians 3:20 AMP)

How would God come through?
Would He come through?

I knew God hadn't brought us this far to fail us now. As I had often heard, and even preached myself, ***"When it's God's will, it's God's bill."*** Now this promise wasn't just a cute, catchy saying. We knew somehow, some way, God would provide. We were desperately depending on it.

God Has His Ways!

A few weeks later we received a call from an organization across the street from our church that we partnered with to feed the community, Metropolitan Ministries. It was a ministry we highly respected and greatly appreciated. They cooked gourmet, hot meals in their commercial kitchen three times a week, and we served them at our church since we had a larger facility. They called to tell us that a local TV station was coming to their center to do an interview about the needs of the homeless in our county. They asked if we would be willing to share the story about the work we were all doing together to feed the community hot meals and also if we would share a little about the boy's story. They were raising funds to build a new housing complex that would assist families to get back on their feet after falling on hard times. We knew about this project and knew our community needed the new facility, so we said "Of course, we'd love to come over and share our story if it will help."

On our way over the news reporter called to discuss what we should expect in the interview. In our conversation she casually asked if we had a GoFundMe account set up for our adoption needs? I told her I hadn't even thought about it. She urged us to take a chance and set one up. She promised, if we did, she would promote the page at the end of our interview.

So, while we were still in the car driving to do the interview, I took out my phone, set up a GoFundMe account and wrote up a quick synopsis about our story. I didn't think much more about it. The interview went well; and on the drive home, I remember being thankful we could raise the awareness of the needs in our community.

I was so excited for their miracle as the community was giving to their project.

I had no idea of the miracle that was about to take place for us. We woke up the next morning totally surprised.

Not only was our story shared on our local news station, but also on news stations all around the world. To our even greater surprise, literally thousands of people had gone to our GoFundMe account and made a donation. In fact, so many people gave, with so much generosity, that within twenty-four short hours, we exceeded our financial goal. God had already done so many miracles, so many times in our lives, and here He was doing it again.

Oh, how I rejoiced in God's goodness. His faithfulness. His provision. What a wonderful miracle He had done for us. I realized this is what it must have felt like for the Israelites after they had been in captivity for hundreds of years, finally returning home.

The Psalmist describes the joy in their journey this way:

When the LORD brought back his exiles to Jerusalem, it was like a dream! We were filled with laughter, and we sang for joy.
And the other nations said, "What amazing things the LORD has done for them."
Yes, the LORD has done amazing things for us! What joy!
Restore our fortunes, LORD, as streams renew the desert.
Those who plant in tears will harvest with shouts of joy.
They weep as they go to plant their seed,
but they sing as they return with the harvest.
Psalm 126 NLT

How About You?

Perhaps you're facing an impossible situation and feel as if God has forgotten you. I want to encourage you and remind you God still performs miracles! Yes, sometimes, actually many times, God does it just in the nick of time; but He still does it!

It's like the movie, "It's A Wonderful Life," when it seemed as if it was all over, it was only the beginning. God had a plan all along. Ronnie and I didn't need to figure it all out. All we needed to do was do what we could do in the natural, then trust God, and He would do the rest in the super-natural.

I felt as if the tide had finally turned. It seemed as if our season of suffering was finally over!

But not quite yet.

Prayer

This prayer is for all my friends that are facing cancer or have friends or family members fighting this disease. Be encouraged. Whether God delivers you from the storm or supernaturally strengthens you to endure; both are miracles, and I want to come into agreement with you for your healing.

Dear God,
I thank you for dying on the cross for me not only to save me, but also I thank you for paying the price for my healing. Lord I come into agreement with Isaiah 53:5 that states by YOUR stripes, I am healed! I am not a victim of cancer, I am an overcomer and a child of God. I lay down the identity of cancer and will not allow that label to be attached to my life. I am who YOU say that I am! I claim my healing and thank you for the grace you have bestowed on my life. I trust YOU with my life, I love YOU, and I will keep my eyes focused on YOU. In Jesus name Amen!

Quotes to Remember:

Courage is like a muscle.
We strengthen it with use.

His eye is on the sparrow and I know he watches me.

For nothing is impossible to God!
Luke 1:37

When it's God's will, it's God's bill.

But he was wounded for our transgressions, he was bruised for our iniquities: the chastisement of our peace was upon him; and with his stripes we are healed.
Isaiah 53:5 KJV

chapter nine

IT'S NOT OVER

The adoption was going smoothly and was on track to be finalized in three weeks. My three-month follow-up appointment with the oncologist also went well. All my results looked great; I was healing from surgery, and I just finally felt as if I was on the mend. Things were looking up, not only for me, but for my whole family. We could finally take a deep breath and look ahead to the future. We could feel that our season of suffering was finally over!

Our kids had been champions through this entire challenging ordeal, so before the adoption became final, Ronnie and I wanted to take some time to relax and reconnect as a family. Although we were overjoyed with all that had been happening, it had been one long, exhaustive, emotional roller coaster ride. Our nerves were shot. We needed a break.

We left for a much-anticipated five-day cruise as a family. Our first stop was in the Bahamas; and, oh, it felt so good to feel that sunshine on my face. We were finally back to living the dream...

Until I woke up on a Sunday morning.

When I woke up I grabbed my phone to check in on social media – something I rarely had the chance to do – I noticed multiple missed calls and texts from my father back in the States. Dad and I were both pranksters, so at first I didn't think much about it. Probably just another one of Dad's pranks. Or perhaps he had even forgotten I was on vacation. I wasn't sure which, so I found a place with cell phone service and called home.

Dad answered on the first ring.

I could tell by his voice this wasn't a prank. Something was terribly wrong. My dad was hysterical and said, "Krystal, your mom died last night. The police and paramedics are here, and I need you to come as fast as you can."

Time stopped.

I was standing on the pool deck of the cruise ship watching everyone laughing, eating their breakfast and sipping their coffee when suddenly it was as if they all disappeared; and I felt totally alone. I could still feel the phone on my ear; and I replied, "Dad, what are you saying?" It was then I heard the words as clear as day, "*Your mom is dead;*" and then I heard him sobbing and knew my life would never be the same.

Within hours I was on a plane heading home to enter the season I can only describe as Shattered.

Our Bond Was Strong

Mom and I were very close. We had both faced our own battles over the years, and had fought hard for one another. Our bond was strong, unbreakable. I couldn't bring myself to even acknowledge she was gone.

I remember growing up watching Mom face one illness after the other. One of the many illnesses my mom had was debilitating migraines. They often got so severe she would have to leave wherever we were and go lie down with an ice pack on her head. She hated missing out on the fun with the family, but the pain made it impossible to stay. I prayed for Mom's migraines to get better, but over the years they only got worse — along with several other illnesses.

I was the youngest of three siblings; and by the time I turned thirteen, I was the only child still living at home. My brother had joined the Air Force and moved away, and my sister had gotten married and moved out. Mom's migraines would sometimes get so severe I would often have to drive her to the hospital since I was the only one still home.

Here's how our routine would often go.

My friend Mike picked me up in the morning and took me to the technical school I attended to become a certified medical assistant. My classes were early in the morning, and all of them were over by eleven. After class I called Mom to see how she was feeling. If she was feeling okay, I would stay at school and do homework before going back home.

If she was sick from one of her migraines, I went home right away to be with her just in case they became severe.

Most days, I needed to go home.

If Mom's migraines were really, really severe, I went home, picked her up and drove her to the hospital in downtown Detroit so that she could get an occipital nerve block in the back of her head, to numb her pain.

Most times, we were at the hospital for hours. If she needed to be admitted, I would leave her there overnight and drive home by myself. Now don't judge...my dad worked full time to pay the bills; and, even though I was only fourteen, I was an amazing driver. I knew the rules for driving in downtown Detroit at night: You slow down at stop signs, stop and look both ways, and go at red lights. And never make eye contact with the car next to you! Dad was on duty for my mom during nights and weekends, and I was on duty for Mom during the day. That worked for us.

Funny story.

Because I was an underage driver, I kept one of my sister's old driver's licenses to use in case I ever got pulled over by the police. Well, one day I did get pulled over for not wearing a seatbelt. I gave the officer my sister's driver's license. He took a look at it, and it worked. He thought I was old enough to drive.

Later, however, when I told my sister she had a seatbelt ticket she would need to pay….well, let's just say she wasn't very happy with me.

If Mom was admitted and I had to stay at the hospital with her, I did my school work in her room or in the waiting room. I'm sure this is where my fascination with wanting to become a doctor started. I thought to myself, "Hmm, since I'm at the hospital more than most of the doctors around here are, I might as well get paid one day for being one!"

Mom told me often that I would make a great doctor. She also encouraged me to be the one who would find a cure for all her illnesses. I would read Mom's diagnostic reports and try to figure out a remedy. I would read every pamphlet in the hospital I could find and study every medical book I came across. I loved talking to the doctors — and I sure wasn't shy about offering them all of my free medical advice.

Fast forward twenty years, and I'm now dealing with the devastating reality that my mom—my hero, my number one supporter—was gone.

Don't Get Your Hopes Up

I had not ever really thought about how heartbreaking it must have been for Joseph to live through the betrayal of his brothers throwing him into a pit, selling him into slavery, miraculously ending up in the palace, and then being falsely accused and thrown back into prison again.

That's how I felt.

Just when it seemed my dreams were coming back to life, the devil was saying,

"Don't get your hopes up. It's not over yet!"

Hope deferred makes the heart sick,
but a dream fulfilled is a tree of life.
Proverbs 13:12 NLT

What strength I had regained after winning my battle with cancer now seemed lost. The pieces I had fought so hard to put back together were coming apart. I was scared. I felt as though I was skydiving without a parachute and didn't have anything left for another fight. I had already just barely been hanging on, but now the cord was cut; and I was free falling.

I honestly didn't even care.

The trauma threw me back into shock. My heart was numb. My mind was a wreck. My body was breaking down. I had found courage to fight cancer, found courage to fight for my marriage, and found courage to fight for my boys; but did I have any courage left?

Could I find my way through another deep wave of grief?

Could I fight my way through another fierce battle?

Could I stumble my way through another dark valley?

I wasn't sure.

The writings in my journal reflect these uncertainties:

When pain floods my heart, I inhale Your love and Live another moment
Your love is my breath
I take Your courage and press on another step
My existence depends on your love. I won't survive a moment without it
Your gift of courage is without price and my life
My dreams come alive in You
This dreamer still believes in miracles
He whispers to my heart and heals my soul.

I remember after my hysterectomy lying in bed one night thinking, "Why do we so easily settle for living on autopilot or simply stumbling along in survival mode? Why is it that we go through the motions of life not realizing how fast it's actually passing us by?"

Now, facing my mom's death, I remembered why.

We often go on autopilot or simply stumble along in survival mode because many times life is just too painful to face. That's what I was facing. Could I go on? Did I even want to go on?

You are strong enough to face it, even if it doesn't feel like it right now.

My heart was telling me I shouldn't. My body was telling me I couldn't. In fact, in the days and months following Mom's death, I was hospitalized twice for heart issues, suffered chronic infections, and broke out in a rash that covered my entire body. I was diagnosed with an autoimmune disease. My body had literally started attacking itself. The unhealthy cells were fighting the healthy ones — and I was just letting it happen. I had spent my entire life fighting for everyone else; yet somewhere along the way, I had stopped fighting for myself. I was now bearing the consequences: physically, mentally, emotionally, and spiritually. My doctors had directly said to me, "Krystal, if you don't start taking care of yourself, you're going to die."

Again, some of my thoughts during that dark season were reflected in my journal:

> To begin again or end the unending,
> pain never releases just changes,
> where else can it go?
> The bottom keeps getting deeper and the top unseen.
> Why start climbing again to be thrown in another pit?
> I have no rope, I need support.
> Please don't let it end this way; something's gotta give,
> can't avoid, have to face but need your grace & mercy.

A U-Turn

A few months before my mom's death, I had been invited to speak at a church for a women's conference. Stupid me. Looking back, I now realize that accepting this ministry engagement probably wasn't the smartest idea. As a result of my hysterectomy, I was still adjusting to my lack of hormones and couldn't string a sane sentence together without bawling like a baby. Those poor ladies had no idea what they were in for.

In preparation to speak, I had gotten up early that morning and gone for a walk on the beach. Since I didn't have any kids with me, plus I had the opportunity to sleep in at a luxury hotel, I kept thinking to myself, "Why are you up so early? Why aren't you taking a rare advantage of getting a few extra hours of sleep? Just go back to bed."

Yet, here I was wide awake sitting on the beach.

It was turtle nesting season, and I could still see fresh marks in the sand where a giant sea turtle had pulled her body all the way from the shore, dug a place to lay her eggs, and then dragged her body back into the water.

It was an unusual sight.

I continued walking, looking for similar tracks in the sand. It was still early in the morning; and the beach was pretty much untouched with footprints, so these huge tracks in the sand made from female turtles the night before were easy to spot.

I was about to head back to my room when I noticed another set of tracks. These tracks were different. They didn't traverse from shore to sand dunes. Instead, they came out of the ocean about ten feet and then right back in.

This unusual U-shaped pattern intrigued me.

I took a picture of these unusual tracks and headed back to

the hotel. When I returned home from the conference, I did some research and discovered that this rare U-shape pattern is called a *false crawl.* Female turtles start their journey of nesting; but when they get distracted by lights or spooked by noise, instead of completing their journey, they just move through the motions.

You are stronger than you think.

Just think about it.

These magnificent creatures journey hundreds of miles back to the very beach where they were born. Then they drag their massive bodies up on the beach to lay their eggs. But if they become too exhausted or get distracted by sights or sounds, they abort their mission and instead, give up, make a U-turn and head back to the ocean.

Each of us were created to "birth things." Whether it's a business, a book, a family, a ministry, a legacy—whatever it may be for you—we were all created to create. Yet so many times, for so many of us, we get too exhausted or too distracted or too scarred from our journey, and start walking in circles — and sometimes we just give up and even stop walking altogether.

The pain of our journeys can cause us to settle for going through the motions, doing a U-turn, and leaving little to nothing behind.

While I was grieving my mom's death, God brought the picture of these *false crawls* of the giant sea turtle back to mind. I realized just how many times I had been okay with going through the motions. Deep down I knew I couldn't continue that way. *I knew I had to let go of everything I couldn't change, and find the courage to face the things I could change.*

It was time for me to surrender it all: all my grief, all my hurts, all my regrets, all my bitterness, all my shame. If I was going to live— really live, literally live — I had to let it all go. If not, I would end up aborting my mission, if not my very life.

Emotional wholeness leads to physical wholeness.

All of us can get away with holding on to things and carrying extra baggage for a while. We can push our emotions down, cover up our pain, and hide our hurts. But God wouldn't let me do it any longer. He said, "Enough is enough! It's time to lay them all down." God, in His kindness, used my physical illnesses and forced me to face my emotional sickness. I could no longer carry the grief, the pain, the sorrow, the regret, the shame, the humiliation, the anger. My body couldn't carry it any longer — and neither could I.

I'm well aware that among many churches much of the focus is solely on physical healing. And while I believe in physical healing—and I thank God daily I experienced that Miracle with my cancer—I also believe we need to focus on emotional and mental healing. I believe emotional wholeness leads to physical wholeness.

When we truly allow our souls to heal, our bodies will follow. Granted, it takes a lot of courage to face the true state of our soul. Whether that's the courage to forgive others, forgive ourselves, letting others go, and letting go of the things you cannot change, it's when we do focus on the health and healing of our soul that brings the most reward.

And that's what God was doing in my life.

Little did I know that in my surrender I would gain one of my greatest weapons; I would be introduced to my true self. Not who others wanted me to be, or who I thought I should be, but who God had made me to be. In my surrender, I found my real self. My true identity as a daughter accepted and loved by the Father.

While my story is filled with physical and financial miracles, it's the emotional wholeness I'm most thankful for. God healed my heart and gave me the courage to be who I am today: a woman strong enough to face her pain and find healing in His presence.

I now know why God allowed physical sickness to enter my story. Don't misunderstand me: I know that sickness and suffering is not the only way God molds people. And I am not saying God caused my sickness. He didn't.

But He did use it to create something beautiful in me.

It's hard to put into words how God revealed himself to me during this season. I started experiencing how much God loved me, really loved me — just for me. I began to understand that the true me was all God had ever wanted me to be. It was never about my identity as a pastor's wife, a mother, a daughter, a speaker, a writer — it was always and only about ME.

He didn't love me for what I did; He loved me for who I was. He was the One who created me exactly the way He wanted me to be; and because He was the One who created me, I was good enough for

Him. And if I was good enough for Him, then the "real me" was good enough for me.

So often in my life I had felt like such a failure for every title I'd ever held. I felt as if I'd let everyone down. But when I was at my lowest and had nothing to offer, God didn't discard me. He picked me up and carried me. In my brokenness, God still wanted me. Oh, what unimaginable, endless, unconditional love.

Restoration

During this time of my own self-discovery, God led me into restoring furniture. I would find old thrift store pieces that at one time had been someone's very special treasure, but they were now discarded and left as trash. Because of my own place of brokenness I could easily see the beauty in these damaged pieces. What people saw as trash I saw as treasure.

After my mom's passing, my body was still in shock; and I was very fragile. Actually, more than fragile, I was broken. I could barely look someone in the eye or carry on a conversation, much less have the clarity of mind to write or the confidence to preach. I also had terrible insomnia, and restoring furniture gave me something to do. So I would sit for hours at night, all by myself, restoring furniture, and crying.

I couldn't help wondering how much time Jesus had worked on furniture, in his father's carpentry shop, all alone. Was this perhaps when Jesus discovered His true identity as well? Was this perhaps when Jesus gained the courage He would need once He revealed Himself to the world? There's no way to know for sure, but I'd like to think so.

When I worked on restoring furniture, I felt Jesus' gentle hands, lovingly and patiently restoring me.

My journal once again reflects the restoration Jesus was working in my life:

You found me...
Awaken dreamer, dare to dream again...
This is your appointed time to let things live and let things die
Bring me back to life again (Furniture) each piece has a story to tell...
Your time is not over yet, you're just being renovated, refurbished, and if you allow yourself to be restored and live again;
My story is not over yet;
It's just a different chapter now, not a new book.
One time to live + now is your time
Find the courage to Live
No going through the motions (turtle).

It's NOT Over

My mom, fifteen years before her death, had been in a car accident, which left her with many chronic health problems. But she was a fighter; and thankfully she was, because she had over thirty-three surgeries and close to a hundred hospitalizations over her lifetime.

Even though Mom was a Christian and believed in healing, she lived in so much chronic pain that she would often ask God to take her home. She was ready to go. She was waiting to go.

There had been several times when she was battling life-threatening illnesses or facing massive surgeries and almost died.

But Mom always experienced a miracle.

Mom had such faith in God that she knew when the enemy wanted to take her, she wouldn't die. She would only go home when God wanted to take her home.

Mom's prayer was finally answered.

As she slept, her body shut down; and she was gently taken home. All her tears, all her fears, all her pain... gone, resting in the Father's arms.

Laurel M. Ash

August 3, 1955 - July 24, 2016

The day after my mom's death, something very unusual happened: an unexpected package showed up on her front doorstep. Mom loved shopping online and was always receiving packages in the mail, but this one was different. It was two bracelets she had ordered from China a few months earlier, of course having no idea when they might arrive.

But here they were: two bracelets arriving on her doorstep the day after her death, with these special words written on them,

"My story is not over yet!"

My mom's story is not over. She's in Heaven rejoicing with the Author of all stories. And neither is my story finished. I'm still on a journey — a courageous, exciting, adventurous journey. And your story, well, your story is not over yet either!

If you are in a season right now where it feels as though you are going through hell, I want to encourage you again... KEEP GOING! Regardless of how many waves may have hit you, I can promise you every storm eventually runs out of rain. I have always been the one who has been the hardest on myself. I was the goal-setter with big dreams to change the world. I wish I could tell you I was courageous every day and never lost hope, but unfortunately that is not the truth. There were days I was too weak to get out of bed. There were days where, for me, conquering the world was simply taking a shower. Setting a goal for the next week seemed impossible as I was just trying to survive the day. After my mom passed away I put my hair up in a ponytail to get to work! I had a funeral to plan, clothes to pick out, and everyone to fix. I was so determined to get through this season of grief as quickly as I could. I read a book on the 5 steps of grief and found every scripture on grieving and read them on my plane flight home from the Bahamas, thinking I could just go through the motions. It was not until three weeks had passed when I realized I had again forgotten to take care of myself. It was a rude awakening to take my hair out of that bun and see half of it still in the ponytail holder. My long, luscious "Barbie Locks" were gone… Even in my greatest battles I was trying to prove to everyone I was good enough. Holding my hair in my hand was when I knew I had to surrender. Growing up as an athlete, I have always been very competitive and had compared surrendering to losing. God taught me so graciously that it was actually the opposite. The moment I gave up doing it my way was the moment God could finally take over.

Our God is a great, good, gracious, and faithful God! And because He is, I want to encourage you to claim your courage. Know that He is with you every step of the way. Know that by God's grace you CAN DO THIS. Know that by God's grace, you are STRONG ENOUGH and by His grace, you are GOOD ENOUGH.

He never said the journey would be easy, but He did say, in the end, it would be worth it. So keep fighting. God is with you. God is for you. God deeply loves you!

Your story is not over yet!
So do not throw away your confidence;
it will be richly rewarded.
Hebrews 10:35 NIV

I want to give you an opportunity to pray one more time with me. This time I am going to leave some blank spaces for you to fill in. I promise, God wants to hear from you, even if it feels as if it's not pretty. I want you to be honest; those are His favorite conversations.

PRAYER

Hey God it's ______(Insert Name)________,

I know it has been awhile since I told you how I feel, and I am so sorry for taking so long. Thank you for sitting by me in my pit until I was ready to get out… Today, I'm ready to let go of ____________(Past Hurts)______________I surrender!

I've been so __________(Angry, Hurt, Ashamed?)________________.

I am sorry for not trusting you with ___________(Struggles)_____________

I am ready to let go and give you control.

Forgive me for ________________________________ and I choose to forgive myself for ______________________________________.

I choose from this day forward to trust you, NO MATTER WHAT! I love you and thank you for loving me even when I felt unlovable. I choose to believe you have plans for me and they are GOOD. I choose to surrender my life to you.

Love,

_______________Your Name_______________

Quotes to Remember:

You have to face your own battles before you can fight for others.

You are stronger than you think you are.

Emotional wholeness leads to physical wholeness.

Your story is not over yet.

People saw trash, yet I saw treasure.

So do not throw away your confidence; it will be richly rewarded.
Hebrews 10:35

ACKNOWLEDGEMENTS

At the beginning or ending of every book there is a very important page that most people typically skip over and I believe it is the page that tells you THE MOST about the author. No, I am not talking about the typical "Author" page, or "About Me" paragraph. That's the info they want you to know about them. If you really want to get to know an author, go and read their personal Acknowledgments page. This is the page where the author takes the time, or doesn't, to publicly thank those that have contributed to their success. The truth is... no one becomes anyone, or produces anything, without someone contributing something to their life. Good or bad. Does that make sense? So without further ado I want to take the time to thank the academy... Just kidding, that's not until next year.

And again, without further ado
here goes mine...

Courage to Live:

First and foremost I would not be alive Physically, Mentally, or Spiritually without the courage that was offered to me by Jesus Christ. He gave me the courage to truly live, and I took it. Thank you.

Courage to Love:

Ronnie, you have taught me that love never fails even when we think it has. You may be the most positive person on this entire PLANET! My life changed the second I laid my eyes on you and I am forever grateful for your love. You are my Peetie…forever. <3

Ronnie III, your compassion has challenged me to my core. Your ability to empathize with others and in turn have the Godly wisdom to encourage them is a gift. Thank you for the many times you have encouraged me. I love you so much an can't wait to see all the great things God has in store for your life! The best is yet to come!

Riley, your drive to follow your dreams has reminded me of the beauty of dreaming. You are incredibly smart, wise, and I believe you will accomplish all that you have set your mind to. You have taught me how to be strong, yet kind. Thank you for helping me edit my first rough draft in a fancy coffee shop and then late in the night at the creepy McDonalds we were almost kidnapped at (true story). You were my biggest fan, and I will always be yours. I love you my Rie Pie!

Selah Rae, you command every room you desire with your wit and humor. You make me smile as you do everyone that comes in contact with you. You are such a great friend that loves buying everyone gifts! Your friends are lucky to have you in their life as am I. You're so thoughtful and thank you for removing my makeup when I'm too tired in bed. Thank you for being you and having a heart of gold. You are so smart, love you my sweet girl.

Dallas, my little helper. Your laughter has a way of filling up everyone around you, it's contagious! You absolutely love talking to people, regardless of who they are. You love Jesus and love praying for me at night. Thank you for being so strong and teaching me how to overcome challenges. I love you my precious, caring boy!

Grayson, the boss. You love being the boss, even if it's just over Winston (the dog). You have a way of being so honest it's amazing to hear your thoughts. Thank you for your sweetness and love. I can't imagine my life without you in it. Keep wearing the tie, you are going to do great things and change the world! You're my little buddy forever!

My dad, one of my greatest encouragers. In the midst of such pain you have faced you still find a way to focus on making the lives of others better. Thank you for choosing the better over the bitter and showing me I can do the same. I'm so grateful to have you as my father and I love you dearly. And Shirley, thank you for loving my father so well and taking care of him… we all know he needs it, MR 1953…We love you Shirley!

My mom, although you are not here in the present your love and wisdom carries on everyday in my heart. There's not a single day that passes that I'm not reminded of the beautiful legacy you left behind. Thank you for loving me.

My sister, Jaime, you love so deeply. Thank you for being so caring and nurturing. I love that people tell me we laugh the same because I love you!

My big brother, York, as a little girl I looked to you as my hero. You are brave, strong, and a fighter and I still see those same qualities in you. Thank you for never giving up and I believe the best is yet to come for you!

Mom and Dad Stewart, Thank you for accepting me as one of your own from the beginning. I have learned so much from the both of you and continue to be inspired by your love for God, your family, and the church. Thank you for your constant encouragement and support.

Tony & Kaci, Justin & Jaime - Thanks for the many laughs at all the family dinners! Honestly you have all inspired me in so many ways as I have watched you overcome your own life's challenges. You are all miracles that I admire... Love you brothers and sisters!

To all my nieces and nephews, You are world changers! I love watching you all grow and find your own paths. God has great plans for you and it's an honor to be on the bleachers cheering you on! Also Kenzie... Thank you for taking my cover photo at midnight... fun times and LOTS of pants. Love you all!

My besties 4 the resties - Sarah, Kate, Bri, Bean, Cassie, Amy you are truly a gift of friendship. A friend that sticks closer than a brother. I love you all dearly and still can't believe I'm so blessed to have 6 of the strongest, smartest, best friends. And Bean thanks for all the hours you assisted me with editing! I didn't realize how lucky I was to have you all until I grew up and realized everyone didn't have friends like you - A book could not contain all the fun memories we have created as teenagers from figure skating, trampoline nights, the car wash, to movie nights that ended with gum in someone's hair. Those fun memories have carried us through the pain and grief we have also shared together as life continued to change. You all inspire me, my courageous friends…

Courage to Write:

Lindsay Roberts, you gave me the courage to start writing and along the way God used you to become one of my greatest encouragers during a dark time. Thank you for being a light and staying so sensitive to hear from the Lord and speak words of life over me. Your life gives me courage and I am a life that was forever changed by your YES.

Ken Roberts, my writing coach! Thank you for your patience. Your encouragement has been a gift and I couldn't have completed this book with such excellence without you!

Dr. Paul Zahl, my insecurities would have stopped me from ever speaking with you at the Unleashed Conference and developing a friendship. I'm so glad I didn't know how wonderful you were before we met. Thank you for your constant encouragement.

Amie Dockery, Your writing perfection has inspired me like none other. It has pushed me to go deeper and I love your transparency when you preach. I read Unfollow Your Heart in 2018 and it challenged me to my core. You are clear and precise and hit the target each time. Thank you.

Pastor Sam (Rodriguez), I don't know you well personally, yet feel as if I do after reading You Are Next 2X in 2019, From Survive to Thrive in 2020, and most recently Persevere with Power! You are the real deal and I am inspired by your willingness to speak to the victimhood that holds so many of us back. Instead of running ahead you have taken the time to pause and throw a rope to us that were stuck behind. Thank you.

Courage to Preach:

Pastor Paula White-Cain, my thanks extend many years back as I started out as a young pastor's wife reading your books that inspired me to dream. The first Bible Study I ever taught as a 21 yr old pastor's wife was from your book, "Deal With It!". Thank you for paving a way for so many to unashamedly preach the word of God regardless of the naysayers. Your ability to stand amidst life's ferocious storms and not quit has developed a grit inside me to declare that God had Something Greater for my life, giving up wasn't an option. Thank you for never giving up and continuing to run the race and change the world. Love you!

Pastor Hope Carpenter, I met you once and you bought me a bracelet! You are so generous and make everyone feel like a somebody. Thank you.

Terri Savelle Foy, I attended your Next Conference in the midst of a pit season of my life. You reminded me to keep the dream alive and I did! I made a decision in that season I would take the small steps everyday that would lead me to finish this book and even with 5 kids, a national pandemic, and a new full time career it's amazing what can happen with a made up mind. Thank you for who you are - you are making a difference!

Ashton Parsley, your willingness to be transparent and share your personal testimony of depression changed me. You are so brave, so bold, and millions of lives have been impacted by it. Thank you.

Christine Martin, Thank you for being so authentic and preaching the Word with such authority. You are a prophetic gift and I an so grateful for you!

And last but not least my incredible publishing company, Two Penny Publishers, I couldn't have done this without you… literally! But seriously Jodi Costa and Jessica Conley you are the best! Let's do another one!

NOTE FROM THE AUTHOR

Hey Friends,

Thank you for taking the time to read my written words. 26 letters formatted in as many different ways as I could possibly think of to share my journey with you. My greatest prayer is that by sharing my story with you it has brought you courage. And now I'm going to ask you to think of someone that needs that same courage right now and to give them this book... Yes, give this book away! You can buy another one if you'd like, or five, or ten more to give away! If someone is going through a hard time you cannot give them faith, but you can give them courage. I know my story will be different from what they are facing but believe me.. As a book reader myself, I can tell you I have found courage in some of the most unlikely places.

Let's change the world by encouraging one person at a time!

Love you friends and also come find me on social media! I would love to "virtually" meet you and hope we can encourage each other! I would update you right now on how life is currently going, but as you also know, life is ever changing and I can guarantee it will not be relevant by the time you read this. But I can guarantee this, I am still trusting God in all the ups and downs and taking courage everyday. Life is a gift - live it!

Love, Krystal

ABOUT THE AUTHOR

Krystal is a writer, a speaker, and a top-producing Real Estate Agent in the DC/Maryland region.

As a pastor's kid she already knew that people, including Christians, could sometimes misunderstand or even be cruel regarding someone's calling, and her desire to be a "serious" teacher of the Word was quickly deflated when she was given the nickname "Preacher Barbie." Feeling defeated before she even got started, Krystal turned to God looking for a quick escape.

Instead, He reminded her that His ways were higher than her ways and her calling was still her calling. Krystal has been married 20+ years to her pastor husband Ronnie and they have five amazing children. After giving birth to three amazing children Krystal was hit with a cervical cancer report and the need for a hysterectomy. But, as only God would have it immediately following surgery as only God could orchestrate, two beautiful homeless babies were unexpectedly brought into The Stewart's Home, and after a wild process that included news coverage nationwide, they were able to adopt those two beautiful boys and complete their family.

If Krystal has learned one thing throughout the struggles, the highs, the lows, the joys, and the sorrows, she has learned the faithfulness of God's provision, healing virtue, and most of all, His great love. It is Krystal's desire to encourage and minister to people all over the world and share that amazing love of God with anyone who will listen.

You can connect with her on Instagram @KrystalStewart or www.krystalstewart.com

Made in United States
Orlando, FL
11 December 2021